0618530

A TREASURY OF

Christmas
Songs and Carols

A
big
book
of words
and music
for Carols
from all over
the world, with
sections devoted
to Christmas hymns,
solo songs, children's
carols,
rounds and canons

A TREASURY OF

Second Edition

with guitar chords

Illustrations by Rafaello Busoni

Piano arrangements by the editor and Rudolph Fellner

Christmas
Songs and Carols

edited and annotated

by

HENRY W. SIMON

HOUGHTON MIFFLIN COMPANY · BOSTON

ISBN: 0–395–17786–3 Hardbound
ISBN: 0–395–17785–5 Paperbound

The translations from the Czech, *To Bethl'em I Would Go* and *Shepherds Watched Their Flocks by Night* are used by permission of their author and copyright owner, Mary Vojácek Cochrane.

The paraphrase *In the Town* is used by permission of its author and copyright owner, Eleanor Farjeon.

The text of *The Three Ships,* from *The Collected Poems of Alfred Noyes,* copyright 1906, 1934 by Alfred Noyes, published by J. B. Lippincott Company, is used by permission.

The translation *In a Manger,* copyright 1918 by Carl Fischer, Inc., is used by permission.

Olga Paul's translations *Mary on the Mountain, Sleep, O Child of Mine,* and *The Child Jesus* were written for the *Round-the-World Christmas Album,* published and copyrighted by the Edward B. Marks Corporation, and are used by permission.

The melody of *The Holly and the Ivy* as used in this book was originally collected by C. J. Sharp. The copyright owners are Novello and Company, whose permission to use the melody has been obtained.

The following materials come from *The Oxford Book of Carols* and are used by permission of the Oxford University Press: the words for *The Saviour's Work, Pat-a-pan, Eia, Eia,* and *The Kings* (translation only), and both the words and melody of *The Irish Carol, Gloucestershire Wassail,* and *Rocking.*

The words and music of *The Birthday of a King* and the translation of *Lo, How a Rose* are used by arrangement with G. Schirmer, Inc.

Merry Christmas is used by arrangement with Silver Burdett Co., which published the round in *Music the World Sings,* copyright 1952.

The music in this book was hand-drawn throughout by Maxwell Weaner, and the text was stripped into place from acetate proofs.

PRINTED IN THE UNITED STATES OF AMERICA

M   15 14 13 12 11

PREFACE

THE FESTIVAL of Christmas is tinged with all the varied emotions best expressed in music. Wonder and awe, gaiety and warmth, generosity, love, happiness, and the thrill of hope—these are the colors the heart paints, these are the songs the voices sing. Tragedy is absent; and yet there is the high seriousness of the season and of its story which lends an emotional depth no other happy festival can have.

It is perhaps for these reasons that the music of Christmas has a character of its own—so exclusively its own, indeed, that it seems far more absurd to sing Christmas songs out of season than to sing any others throughout the year. By the same token, no other season can boast a literature of song half so rich, half so intimately associated with one time and one time only.

And because music, of all art forms, is the most evocative, all of us brought up in the Western tradition must associate certain carols, certain tunes with our childhoods. Christmas is the time when everyone has always heard music—and the same music. It is the time when people who never sing the rest of the year join in with family groups, with school and church groups, with community groups in "Silent Night," "It Came Upon a Midnight Clear"—or maybe only "Jingle Bells."

It is the family groups that I have had in mind in making the present collection. There are plenty of little paperbound collections of carols, or Christmas sections in hymnals, for the use of more or less formal groups who sing in four parts. But there is not in print, so far as I know, any generous-sized collection of Christmas songs and carols, with big type and gay colors, which will invite the whole family to gather round and peer over the local pianist's shoulders as they join in song. Fine and learned anthologies of carols there are, and excellent texts and choir books, but nothing (again, so far as I know; and I have looked hard) made primarily to be attractive and practically usable for a family group, and to include a generous selection of many types of Christmas songs.

There is, I trust, nothing formal about this book. I have included all kinds of material, the one criterion being that this is the sort of music people like to sing at Christmas time. I have tried—and hope I have succeeded—to include all the really universal favorites, a good percentage of those that the ordinary mortal has heard and liked but cannot quite remember the words or tunes to, and a number of comparatively little-known ones from all over the world. A very few have been especially concocted for this book—largely in the last section, "Rounds and Canons," the only division for which there was not an embarrassment of riches to select from.

In standard collections of carols, one almost always finds four-part vocal arrangements adapted somewhat awkwardly for the piano. They are not much fun to play. Those in this book were designed to give the pianist a bit of fun too, though he is always obliged to help out the voices by playing the melody. Practically all of the arrangements for the piano are new, but in the more familiar carols the traditional harmonies are conservatively adhered to. Mr. Fellner and I did our best to keep them easy enough for a mediocre pianist without sacrificing musical interest. The test each had to pass was that I had to be able to play it without practising. That is a pretty severe test; for though I am reasonably fluent with a fiddle, my piano instruction was stopped when as a little boy I showed no talent for the instrument, and I have not practised since.

I have tried to put into the annotations the sort of information that I have always been curious to have about any music or poem I read and too seldom am able to get without digging it out. I have put down only whatever I thought amusing or useful in the way of helping to interpret the spirit of a song. Perhaps I should not have intruded this gossip on the page itself but kept it for an appendix. But I know that in almost any group there is likely to be at least one fellow who cannot keep a tune and who is best kept busy reading to himself. If they have no other merit, these notes may at least keep him quiet and contented.

Mr. Busoni's illustrations I find delightfully varied and full of life. He is an old friend of mine, and when I asked whether he might be interested, I felt obliged to warn him that I thought the job almost impossible. "You will really hate it before you are through," I said. "Just imagine—over thirty lullabies, dozens of Magi, and I don't know how many angels and shepherds." Oddly, it seemed to me, this did not worry him a bit, and it was not till I saw his sketches that I knew why. A good artist, as I should have known, can compose themes and variations without end.

Many friends have helped me with one or many details of the work of collecting, research, translation, and arrangement, but there are a few I want particularly to thank. They include Miss Helen Phillips of Houghton Mifflin's editorial department, who executed a difficult asignment in copy-reading with extraordinary care, dispatch, and tact; Mrs. Casimir Wierzynski, Miss Joyce Chang, and Dr. Louis Goranin, who enabled me to make translations from languages I do not begin to understand; Miss Lois Friedlander, a first-rate musician who has successfully disguised herself as a most efficient and thoughtful secretary; and, above all, my wife, who has listened with patience to many versions of the same carol over and over again, copied out endless stanzas, and consistently lent courage and cheer at every step.

H.W.S.

CONTENTS

CAROLS FROM FOREIGN PARTS

CHRISTMAS HYMNS AND CHORALES

ESPECIALLY FOR CHILDREN

British
and
American Carols

Deck the Halls
with
Boughs of Holly

Traditional Welsh
Gaily

Traditional Welsh
H.W.S.

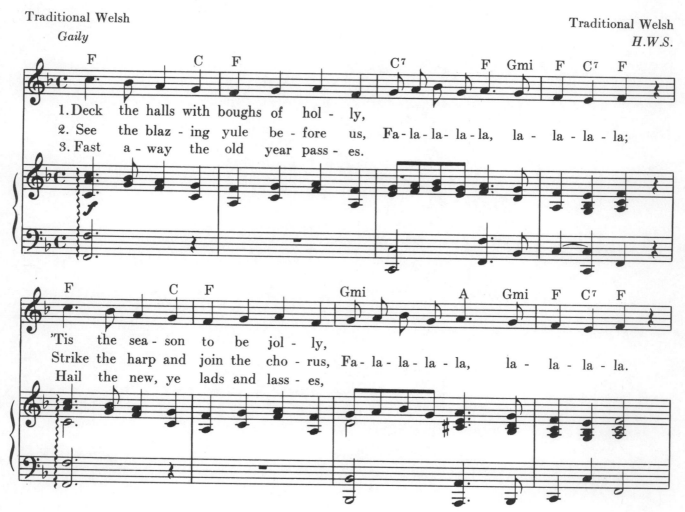

1. Deck the halls with boughs of hol - ly,
2. See the blaz - ing yule be - fore us, Fa - la - la - la - la, la - la - la - la;
3. Fast a - way the old year pass - es.

'Tis the sea - son to be jol - ly,
Strike the harp and join the cho - rus, Fa - la - la - la - la, la - la - la - la.
Hail the new, ye lads and lass - es,

Don we now our gay ap-par-el,
Fol-low me in mer-ry mea-sure, Fa-la-la, fa-la-la, la-la-la.
Sing we joy-ous songs to-geth-er,

Troll the an-cient Christ-mas car-ol,
While I tell of Christ-mas trea-sure, Fa-la-la-la-la, la-la-la-la!
Heed-less of the wind and weath-er,

with octaves ad lib. _ _ _ _ _ _ _ _ _ _ _ _ _ _

THIS IS the most familiar of the Welsh carols and one of the gayest of all carols. Its history is obscure—but it had traveled far enough by the 18th century for Mozart to use it in a duet for violin and piano.

A CHILD THIS DAY IS BORN

Traditional English

Traditional English
R.F.

Firmly

1. A child this day is __ born, A child of high re - nown, Most
2. These tid - ings shep - herds __ heard, In field watch - ing their fold, Were

wor - thy of a scep - ter, A scep - ter and a crown:
by an an - gel un - to them That night re - vealed and told: Now -

				B	C	B		D		Emi	Ami	D	G	C

ell, Now - ell,   Now - ell,   Now - ell, sing all ___ we may,   Be -

	C	Ami	F	D⁷	C		C⁷	Dmi	C	Cdim	C	G	C

cause the King of all _____ kings Was born this bless - ed day.

3. To whom the angel spoke,
   Saying, "Be not afraid;
   Be glad, poor silly shepherds—
   Why are you so dismayed?

4. "For lo! I bring you tidings
   Of gladness and of mirth,
   Which cometh to all people by
   This Holy Infant's birth":

5. Then was there with the angel
   An host incontinent
   Of heavenly bright soldiers,
   Which from the Highest was sent:

6. Lauding the Lord of God,
   And his celestial King;
   All glory be in Paradise,
   This heavenly host did sing:

7. And as the angel told them,
   So to them did appear;
   They found the young Child, Jesus Christ
   With Mary, His mother dear:

THE EARLIEST known publication of this carol occurs in William Sandys' *Christmas Carols, ancient and modern, including the most popular in the West of England, with the tunes to which they are sung*. The date was 1833, and twenty-one stanzas were given. With the refrain repeated each time, this called for forty-two repetitions of the eight-bar tune. It is a good tune, but it would seem that seven stanzas and fourteen repetitions ought to be plenty for anyone. And if even that seems like too much of a good thing, it is suggested the refrain be sung only before the first and after the last stanza.

In Sandys, the title of the carol is given as *Novels*, and the first line of the refrain was printed, "Novels, novels, novels." The meaning intended may have been either "Nowell" (which is how we print it, following other modern editors) or—more meaningfully—"news." The use of "silly" to describe the shepherds in the third stanza suggests a fairly early date for the carol. In Shakespeare's time the word, like the German *selig*, still meant "blessed."

The First Nowell

Traditional

Traditional
- *H.W.S.*

1. The first Now - ell, the an - gel did say, Was to
2. They look - ed up and saw a star Shin - ing

cer - tain poor shep-herds in fields as they lay; In fields where
in the east, be - yond them far, And to the

they lay keep-ing their sheep, On a cold win - ter's night that
earth it gave great light, And so it con - tin - ued both

6

was __ so deep.
day __ and night. Now - ell, __ Now - ell, Now - ell, Now -

ell, Born is the King __ of Is - ra - el.

3. And by the light of that same star
   Three wisemen came from country far;
   To seek for a King was their intent,
   And to follow the star wherever it went.
   Refrain:

4. This star drew nigh to the northwest,
   O'er Bethlehem it took its rest;
   And there it did both stop and stay,
   Right over the place where Jesus lay.
   Refrain:

5. Then did they know assuredly
   Within that house the King did lie;
   One enter'd it them for to see,
   And found the Babe in poverty.
   Refrain:

6. Then entered in those wisemen three,
   Full reverently upon the knee,
   And offered there, in His presence,
   Their gold and myrrh and frankincense.
   Refrain:

7. Between an ox-stall and an ass,
   This Child truly there He was;
   For want of clothing they did him lay
   All in a manger, among the hay.
   Refrain:

8. Then let us all with one accord
   Sing praises to our heav'nly Lord;
   That hath made heaven and earth of naught,
   And with His blood mankind hath bought.
   Refrain:

9. If we in our time shall do well,
   We shall be free from death and hell;
   For God hath prepared for us all
   A resting place in general.
   Refrain:

WORDS and music were first printed, so far as we know, in the 1833 collection of William Sandys, though there is good reason to suppose that the carol is at least two hundred years older and that it may have originated in France. Sandys' version was somewhat distorted metrically. Subsequent editors have smoothed out most of it nicely; and we print the words and music as they are always sung today—with this exception: we have restored three stanzas usually omitted. You will, accordingly, have to supply your own metrical distortions in a few places in stanzas 5, 7, and 9. You will probably find it an amusing puzzle.

A DAY OF JOY AND FEASTING

A group of high-school children
Festively

Traditional English
R.F.

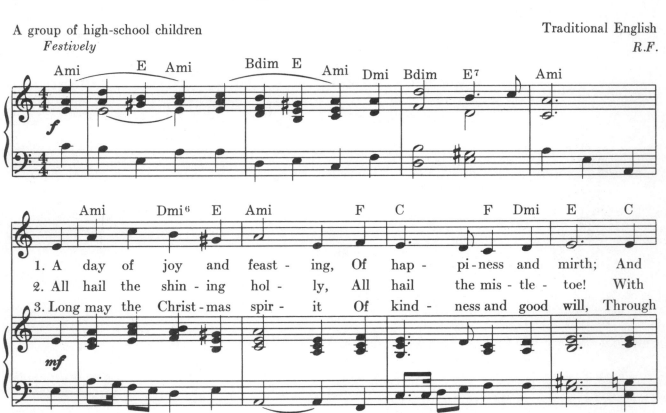

1. A day of joy and feast-ing, Of hap - pi-ness and mirth; And
2. All hail the shin-ing hol - ly, All hail the mis - tle - toe! With
3. Long may the Christ-mas spir - it Of kind - ness and good will, Through

ev - ery year it com - eth here To _ glad - den all the earth.
car - ol gay, all hail the day That com - eth o'er the snow! Sing
joy and pain with us re - main Our hearts with warmth to fill!

No - well! Sing No - well! And _ mer - ry be al - way; _____ Join

in the song, the sound pro - long All on a Christ - mas day.

THE TUNE is remarkably like *The Saviour's Work* (see p. 28) and must date from about the same time. Under the leadership of their English and music teachers, Percival Chubb and Peter Dykema, a group of tenth-graders concocted this carol out of it in 1902. The result is, perhaps, less poetic, but distinctly more gay and festal.

God Rest You Merry, Gentlemen

Traditional English
Unhurried

Traditional English
R.F.

1. God rest you mer-ry, gen-tle-men, Let noth-ing you dis-may, Re-
2. In Beth-le-hem in Jew-ry This bless-ed Babe was born, And

mem-ber Christ our Sav-iour Was born on Christ-mas Day; To
laid with-in a man-ger, Up-on this bless-ed morn; The

save us all from Sa-tan's pow'r When we were gone a-stray
which His moth-er Mar-ry Did noth-ing take in scorn.

O ——

REFRAIN:

10

ti - dings of com - fort and joy, com - fort and joy; O____

ti - dings of com - fort and joy.

3. From God our heav'nly Father
   A blessed angel came;
   And unto certain shepherds
   Brought tidings of the same;
   How that in Bethlehem was born
   The son of God by name.
   Refrain:

4. "Fear not, then," said the angel,
   "Let nothing you affright,
   This day is born a Saviour
   Of a pure Virgin bright,
   To free all those who trust in Him
   From Satan's power and might."
   Refrain:

5. The shepherds at those tidings
   Rejoicéd much in mind,
   And left their flocks a-feeding,
   In tempest, storm, and wind,
   And went to Bethl'em straightway
   This blessed Babe to find.
   Refrain:

6. But when to Bethlehem they came,
   Whereat this Infant lay,
   They found Him in a manger,
   Where oxen feed on hay;
   His mother Mary kneeling,
   Unto the Lord did pray.
   Refrain:

7. Now to the Lord sing praises,
   All you within this place,
   And with true love and brotherhood
   Each other now embrace;
   This holy tide of Christmas
   All others doth deface.
   Refrain:

8. God bless the ruler of this house,
   And send him long to reign,
   And many a merry Christmas
   May live to see again;
   Among your friends and kindred
   That live both far and near—
   And God send you a happy new year, happy new year,
   And God send you a happy new year.

"GENTLEMEN, may God keep you in good spirits," is the meaning of the first line; and good folk sometimes wonder—even in print—why so jolly a sentiment should be sung in a minor key. But the tune is not really in minor; it is simply in one of the old modes. You can call it the Hypodorian mode (according to the system of Gregory the Great) or the Aéolian (according to the system of Gloreanus). All this means, practically, is that you can play the melody on the white keys of the piano if you begin with A. If the tune were really in the modern minor, the first note of the lines "Let nothing you dismay" and "Was born on Christmas Day" would have to be a half tone higher—and the whole feeling of the melodic line would be subtly changed.

Dickens made good use of the opening lines in *A Christmas Carol.* When Scrooge hears them sung, he threatens the anonymous caroler with a ruler. Scrooge could not bear to let nothing him dismay.

I SAW THREE SHIPS

Traditional English

Gaily

FOR ALL ODD-NUMBERED STANZAS

Traditional English
R.F.

1. I saw three ships come sail - ing in, On Christ - mas Day, on Christ - mas Day; I saw three ships come sail - ing in, On Christ - mas Day in the morn - ing.

3. The Vir - gin Mary and Christ were there, On Christ - mas Day, on Christ - mas Day; The Vir - gin Mary and Christ were there, On Christ - mas Day in the morn - ing.

5. O they sailed into Bethlehem,
On Christmas Day, on Christmas Day;
O they sailed into Bethlehem,
On Christmas Day in the morning.

7. Then let us all rejoice amain,
On Christmas Day, on Christmas Day;
Then let us all rejoice amain,
On Christmas Day in the morning.

FOR ALL EVEN-NUMBERED STANZAS

2. And what was in those ships all three, On Christ-mas Day, on Christ-mas Day? And

4. Pray, whith-er sailed those ships all three, On Christ-mas Day, on Christ-mas Day; Pray,

what was in those ships all three, On Christ-mas Day in the morn - ing?

whith-er sailed those ships all three, On Christ-mas Day in the morn - ing?

6. And all the bells on earth shall ring,
On Christmas Day, on Christmas Day;
And all the bells on earth shall ring,
On Christmas Day in the morning.

THE WORDS and music, which have been printed anonymously in England ever since carols were first printed there, is probably at least five hundred years old. It comes in many versions, all of them apparently inspired by the old legend that three mysterious ships sail by "on Christmas Day in the morning." Alfred Noyes's poem "The Three Ships" (see p. 52) is based on the same legend. In this older ballad the ships, instead of carrying gifts for the Child Jesus, bear members of the holy family itself. Sometimes Joseph comes along on the outing, sometimes not. One of the older versions closes with a stanza that expresses the delight of the occasion with charming informality:

O, he did whistle and she did sing,
And all the bells on earth did ring.
For joy that our Saviour He was born
On Christmas Day in the morning.

When the song is sung by a group, it is suggested that the odd-numbered stanzas be sung by the male voices, the even-numbered by treble voices, reflecting the question-answer pattern of the ballad. Everyone can join in the final stanza. Should the pianist find the arrangement of the even-numbered stanzas a little confusing, he can safely use the other throughout.

Baloo, Lammy

Traditional Scottish

Traditional Scottish
R.F.

This day ___ to ___ you ___ is born ___ a ___ Child Of

Ma - ry ___ meek, ___ the Vir - gin ___ mild. That bless - ed

bairn, ___ so lov - ing and ___ kind, Shall now ___ re -

joice ___ both heart ___ and ___ mind. Ba - loo, ___ Lam - my.

THE LULLABY dates approximately from the turn of the 17th century and is also sung to secular words. The rhythm of the seventh measure, and of the others like it, is quite characteristic of its national origin.

GOOD KING WENCESLAS

John Mason Neale (1818–1866)

Piae Cantiones, 1582

H.W.S.

1. Good King Wen - ces - las looked out, On the feast of Ste - phen,
2. "Hith - er, page, and stand by me, If thou knows't it tell - ing,
3. "Bring me flesh, and bring me wine, Bring me pine - logs hith - er:

When the snow lay round a - bout, Deep and crisp and e - ven.
Yon - der peas - ant, who is he? Where and what his dwell - ing?"
Thou and I shall see him dine, When we bear them thith - er."

WENCESLAS the Holy was a 10th-century ruler of Bohemia who, if an unpleasant note may be intruded, was murdered by his brother Boleslav. However, so good were his deeds that he was later canonized. His errand of mercy, charmingly though inconclusively reported in this carol by the learned Dr. Neale, was perhaps one of his minor good deeds, as was his consideration for the page.

The oldest printed version of the tune, found in the 16th-century *Piae Cantiones,* makes a spring song of it, the text beginning, *Tempus adest floridum.* Various authorities, including the editors of the excellent *Oxford Book of Carols,* urge that the tune be returned to its original use; but Christmas without the good Duke Wenzel (he lived before the Pope had elevated rulers to the title of "King") would seem incomplete.

In group singing, the part of the King is often sung by the male voices, the part of the page by treble voices, the narrator's by everyone.

Bright-ly shone the moon that night, Though the frost was cru - el,
"Sire, he lives a good league hence, Un - der - neath the moun - tain,
Page and mon - arch, forth they went, Forth they went to - geth - er;

When a poor man came in sight, Gath-'ring win - ter fu - el.
Right a- gainst the for - est fence, By Saint Ag - nes' foun - tain."
Through the rude wind's wild la - ment And the bit - ter weath - er.

4. "Sire, the night is darker now,
   And the wind grows stronger;
   Fails my heart, I know not how;
   I can go no longer."
   "Mark my footsteps, my good page,
   Tread thou in them boldly;
   Thou shalt find the winter's rage
   Freeze thy blood less coldly."

5. In his master's steps he trod,
   Where the snow lay dinted;
   Heat was in the very sod
   Which the Saint had printed.
   Therefore, Christian men, be sure,
   Wealth or rank possessing,
   Ye who now will bless the poor,
   Shall yourselves find blessing.

THE BOAR'S HEAD CAROL

Perhaps by a student at Queen's College, Oxford

Traditional English
H.W.S.

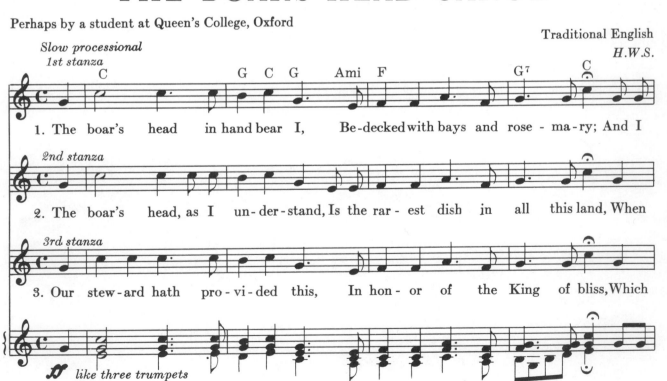

Slow processional

1st stanza

C   G   C G   Ami   F   G⁷   C

1. The boar's head in hand bear I, Be-decked with bays and rose - ma-ry; And I

2nd stanza

2. The boar's head, as I un-der-stand, Is the rar - est dish in all this land, When

3rd stanza

3. Our stew-ard hath pro-vi-ded this, In hon - or of the King of bliss, Which

ff like three trumpets

18

pray you, my mas - ters, be mer - ry, Quot es - tis in con - vi - vi - o:

thus be-decked with a gay gar - land Let us ser - vi - re can - ti- co:

on this day to be ser - ved is, In Re - gi - nen - si a - tri - o:

like a dozen big lutes

REFRAIN: *after each stanza*

Ca - put a - pri de - fe - ro, Red - dens lau - des Do - mi - no.

A LEGEND well over five hundred years old tells us that a student at Queen's College, Oxford, was taking a lonely walk one Christmas morning on a hill near Oxford town when he was attacked by a hungry boar. Otherwise weaponless, the student thrust his copy of a book by Aristotle (legend does not say which one) down the beast's throat, choking him to death. That night the dons and students of the college ate the boar. Every Christmas since then, continues the legend, a boar's head is carried into the hall on a platter, formally placed on the high table, while the carol is sung. The hill where the scholar put Aristotle to valiant use is still called Boar's Hill.

The carol was printed in 1521 by Jan van Wynken de Worde in *Christmasse Carolles*, probably the first volume ever printed in England to contain music.

Here are the meanings of the Latin parts of the macaronic verses:

Quot estis in convivio—as many as are dining together

servire cantico—to serve with a song

In reginensi atrio—in the hall of the Queen

Caput apri defero, reddens laudes Domino—I bring in the boar's head, singing the praises of the Lord.

WHAT SWEETER MUSIC

Robert Herrick (1591-1674)

Johannes Brahms (1833-1897)

Quietly, without dragging

H.W.S.

1. What sweet-er mu-sic can __ we __ bring Than a car-ol
2. O, dark and dull night, fly __ hence a-way And give the hon-or

for to sing The birth of this our heav'n-ly __ King? A-
of this day, That sees De-cem-ber turned __ to __ May; If

wake the voice! A-wake the string! We see Him come and
we may ask the rea-son, say:

REFRAIN:

know — Him — ours, Who with His sun - shine and — His — show'rs Turns

all — the — pa - tient — ground to flow'rs.

3. The darling of the world is come,
   And fit it is we find a room
   To welcome Him. The nobler part
   Of all the house here is the heart:
   Refrain:

4. Which we will give Him, and bequeath
   This holly and this ivy wreath,
   To do Him honor who's our King,
   And Lord of all this revelling:
   Refrain:

THE ENTIRE VOLUME of 1200 poems entitled *Hesperides* (1648) reflects the keen but decorous joy in life and religion of the Devonshire divine, Robert Herrick. His versification had all the skill and delicacy of the contemporary Cavaliers; his attitude toward religion was far more human than that of his other contemporaries, the Roundheads. Both characteristics are delight-fully illustrated in this carol.

So far as I know, Herrick's poem has never had a worthy setting. That is why I have adapted a Brahms melody for it. It comes from the opening of the *String Quintet, Opus 88.* "What sweeter music can we bring?"

Gloucestershire
Wassail

Traditional English

Traditional English
R.F.

Merrily

1. Was - sail,___ Was - sail,___ all o - ver the town!___ Our toast it is
2. So here is to Cher - ry and to his right cheek,___ Pray God send our

white, and our ale __ it __ is brown, Our __ bowl __ it __ is __ made of the
mas - ter a good __ piece __ of beef, And a good __ piece __ of __ beef that __

white ma - ple tree; With the was - sail - ing bowl we'll drink __ to thee.
may we all see; With the was - sail - ing bowl we'll drink __ to thee.

3. And here is to Dobbin and to his right eye,
   Pray God send our master a good Christmas pie,
   And a good Christmas pie that may we all see;
   With our wassailing bowl we'll drink to thee.

4. So here is to Broad May and to her broad horn,
   May God send our master a good crop of corn,
   And a good crop of corn that may we all see;
   With the wassailing bowl we'll drink to thee.

5. And here is to Fillpail and to her left ear,
   Pray God send our master a happy New Year,
   And a happy New Year as e'er he did see;
   With our wassailing bowl we'll drink to thee.

6. And here is to Colly and to her long tail,
   Pray God send our master he never may fail
   A bowl of strong beer; I pray you draw near,
   And our jolly wassail it's then you shall hear.

7. Come, butler, come fill us a bowl of the best,
   Then we hope that your soul in heaven may rest;
   But if you do draw us a bowl of the small,
   Then down shall go butler, bowl and all.

8. Then here's to the maid in the lily white smock,
   Who tripped to the door and slipped back the lock!
   Who tripped to the door and pulled back the pin,
   For to let these jolly wassailers in.

THE WORD *wassail* comes from the Old English *wes hál*, which was a wish of good luck or good health. The word was either a verb, as in this carol, or a noun. The noun refers to the drink—customarily spiced ale. In the third stanza of our carol there appears to be an anticipation of the modern slangy "Here's mud in your eye." (Dobbin is, naturally, a horse in this case; the other friends named are cows.)

The carol has been recorded in Gloucestershire by various English folk-song collectors, including Ralph Vaughan Williams, Cecil Sharp, and others. It dates back at least to the 18th century and is supposed to be sung by a troupe carrying a gaily decorated bowl full of wassail when they begin and possibly refilled several times before they have traveled "all over the town."

NO ROOM IN THE INN

Traditional English

Traditional English
R.F.

1. When Cae - sar Au - gus - tus had __ raised a tax - a - tion, He as -
2. Then Jo - seph and __ Ma - ry, who from Da - vid did spring, __ Went __

sessed all the __ peo - ple that dwelt in the na - tion; The
up to the __ cit - y of Dav - id, their king; ___ And

Jews at that time, be-ing un-der Rome's sway,
there, be-ing en-tered, cold wel-come they find:

peared in the cit-y their trib-ute to pay.
rich to the poor, they are most-ly un-kind.

3. Good Joseph was troubled, but most for his dear,
For her blessed burden whose time now drew near;
His heart with true sorrow was sorely afflicted
That his virgin spouse was so rudely neglected.

4. He could get no houseroom who houses did frame,
But Joseph and Mary must go as they came.
For little is the favor the poor man can find:
From the rich to the poor they are mostly unkind.

5. Whilst the great and the wealthy do frolic in hall,
Possess all the groundrooms and chambers and all,
Poor Joseph and Mary are thrust from the table
In Bethlehem City, ground inhospitáble.

6. And with their mean lodging, contented they be,
For the minds of the just with their fortunes agree;
They bear all affronts with their meekness of mind,
And be not offended though the rich be unkind.

7. O Bethlehem, Bethlehem, welcome this stranger
That was born in a stable and laid in a manger;
For he is a physician to heal all our smarts:
Come welcome, sweet Jesus, and lodge in our hearts.

THE WORDS appeared first in the collection by William Sandys entitled *Christmas Carols, ancient and modern, including the most popular in the West of England . . . 1833*. Only 18 of the carols in this historic collection had tunes printed with them, and *No Room in the Inn* was not among them. Martin Shaw, one of the music editors of the *Oxford Book of Carols*, therefore took one of the tunes that did appear in the book, simplified and invigorated it, and published it in 1928 with his own arrangement for four-part choir. R. F.'s adaptation for voice and piano of Mr. Shaw's adaptation is, naturally, a bit more modern and probably farther from the original in form, though we hope not in spirit.

LULLY, LULLAY

The Coventry Carol

Robert Croo (16th century)

Traditional English
R.F.

3. Herod the king in his raging,
   Chargéd he hath this day
   His men of might, in his own sight
   All children young to slay.

4. Then woe is me, poor Child, for Thee,
   And ever mourn and say,
   For Thy parting nor say nor sing,
   By, by, lully, lullay.

MEDIEVAL GUILDS of many cities of England and the Continent mounted pageants, or "mystery and miracle" plays; and at Christmas time the mystery plays told the story of the birth of Jesus. In 1534 the pageant of the Shearmen and Tailors' Guild included a scene in which the mothers of Jewish children sang this beautiful lullaby after hearing the horrifying order of Herod. The earliest known version of the tune is fifty-seven years younger than the words written by Robert Croo for the pageant. Set down without harmonies and without the tyranny of the bar line, it wavers between common and triple time, between major and minor modes even more than the comparatively recent version now in general use.

The Saviour's Work

Traditional English

Cheerfully and not too slowly

Traditional English
R.F.

1. The Babe in Beth-lem's man-ger laid In hum-ble form so low;
2. A Sav-iour! sin-ners all a-round Sing, shout the wond-rous word;

By won-dering an-gels is sur-veyed Through all His scenes of woe:
Let eve-ry bo-som hail the sound, A Sav-iour! Christ the Lord:

MOST Christmas carols of folk origin deal exclusively with the birth of Jesus, while Easter carols take for their subject His ministry, crucifixion, and resurrection. *The Saviour's Work* is an exception. It was first printed in Staffordshire in 1847 but is probably much older. Not too much, however: the contrasting major and minor suggest a comparatively recent origin for the melody. For a gayer carol with a similar tune, see *A Day of Joy and Feasting* (p. 8).

Now - ell, Now - ell, _____ now _ sing a _ Sav - iour's birth, All hail His com - ing down to earth Who _ rais - es us to _ Heaven!

3. For not to sit on David's throne
   With wordly pomp and joy,
   He came on earth for sin to atone,
   And Satan to destroy:
   Refrain:

4. To preach the word of life divine,
   And feed with living bread,
   To heal the sick with hand benign
   And raise to life the dead:
   Refrain:

5. He preached, He suffered, bled and died
   Uplift 'twixt earth and skies;
   In sinners stead was crucified,
   For sin a sacrifice:
   Refrain:

The Twelve Days of Christmas

Traditional English

Traditional English
R.F.

Gaily

1. On the first day of Christ - mas my true love sent to me A

par - tridge — in a pear tree.

2. On the se-cond
3. On the third day of Christ-mas my true love sent to me
4. On the fourth

Two tur-tle doves and a par-tridge in a pear tree.
Three French hens, (two *etc.*)
Four call-ing birds, (three *etc.*)

repeat as necessary

THE TWELVE DAYS of Christmas lie between Christmas Day and Epiphany, January 6, when the three Magi offered the first Christmas presents—gold, frankincense, and myrrh. This old English cumulative carol is the only folk carol I know which celebrates, in the form of a list, that sometimes fascinating aspect of the season, gift-receiving.

5. On the fifth day of Christ-mas my true love sent to me

Five gold _____ rings!

5-12. Four __ call-ing birds, three French hens,

two __ tur-tle doves, And a par-tridge __ in a pear tree.

Fine

6. On the sixth
7. On the sev-enth
8. On the eighth
9. On the ninth day of Christ - mas my true love sent to me
10. On the tenth
11. On the elev-enth
12. On the twelfth

(Last time)

Six geese a - lay - ing,   Five gold _____ rings!
Sev - en swans a - swim - ming (six *etc.*)
Eight maids a - milk - ing (seven *etc.*)
Nine la - dies danc - ing (eight *etc.*)
Ten lords a - leap - ing (nine *etc.*)
Elev - en pi - pers pi - ping (ten *etc.*)
Twelve drum - mers drum - ming (eleven *etc.*)

repeat as necessary

Go Tell It on the Mountain

Negro Spiritual
Lively

Negro Spiritual
R.F.

1. When I was a seek - er, I sought both night and day, I
2. He made me a watch - man up - on the cit - y wall, And

sought the Lord to help me, and He showed me the way,
if I am a Chris - tian, I am the least of all. Oh!

March time (a little slower)

Go tell it on the moun - tain, o - ver the hills and

Ami   F   Bbmaj⁷   F   Bb

ev' - ry - where,   Go   tell   it   on   the   moun - tain   that

F   Gmi⁷   C⁷   F

Je - sus   Christ __ is   born!

WHEN THIS SPIRITUAL is sung by a leader, with the whole group joining in only on the refrain, it is customary to sing the first part more slowly than the second. When done by one singer or a group in unison, it is more effective to reverse the tempi, as we have done. The important thing—as with all Negro spirituals—is to feel the basic rhythm and to let the melody sing around it, almost in an improvisatory fashion.

Masters in This Hall

William Morris (1834–1896)

Old French

R.F.

1. Mas - ters in   this Hall___   Hear ye news to- day ___
2. Go - ing o'er the hills, ___ Through the milk-white snow, ___

Brought from o - ver seas,___   And ev - er   I   you pray:
Heard I ewes ___ bleat ___ While   the wind   did blow:

Now - ell! Now - ell! Now - ell! Now - ell sing we clear! Hol - pen
are all folk on earth, __ Born __ is God's son so dear:

3. Shepherds many an one
   Sat among the sheep,
   No man spake more word
   Than they had been asleep:
   Refrain:

4. Quoth I, "Fellows mine,
   Why this guise sit ye?
   Making but dull cheer,
   Shepherds though ye be?"
   Refrain:

5. "Shepherds should of right
   Leap and dance and sing,
   Thus to see ye sit,
   Is a right strange thing":
   Refrain:

6. Quoth these fellows then,
   "To Bethlem town we go,
   To see a mighty lord
   Lie in manger low":
   Refrain:

7. "How name ye this lord,
   Shepherds?" then said I.
   "Very God," they said,
   "Come from Heaven high":
   Refrain:

8. Then to Bethlem town
   We went two and two,
   And in a sorry place
   Heard the oxen low:
   Refrain:

9. Therein did we see
   A sweet and goodly may
   And a fair old man,
   Upon the straw she lay:
   Refrain:

10. And a little Child
    On her arm had she,
    "Wot ye who this is?"
    Said the hinds to me:
    Refrain:

11. Ox and ass him know,
    Kneeling on their knee,
    Wondrous joy had I
    This little babe to see:
    Refrain:

12. This is Christ the Lord,
    Masters be ye glad!
    Christmas is come in,
    And no folk should be sad:
    Refrain:

THE TUNE was given by the organist of the cathedral of Chartres to Edmund Stedding, the English carol compiler, who showed it to William Morris, poet, painter, business partner of Rossetti, Burne-Jones, and Ford Madox Ford, and inventor of the Morris chair. His intense interest in folk and Middle English literatures is reflected in the vigorous verses he wrote for the vigorous tune.

For a canonic arrangement of the melody, see page 230.

Now - ell! Now - ell! Now - ell! Now - ell sing we loud! God to -

day hath poor folk raised ___ And ___ cast a - down the proud.

A Babe Is Born

Traditional English
Very simply

Traditional English
R.F.

1. A Babe is born all of a may In the sa - va - sy - oun of _ us. To
Him we sing both night and _ day Ve - ni cre - a - tor Spi - ri - tus.

2. At Beth - le - hem, that bless - ed place, The Child of bliss now born He _ was; And
Him to serve God give us _ grace, O lux be - a - ta Tri - ni - tas.

3. There came three kings out of the east,
   To worship the King that is so free,
   With gold and myrrh and frankincense,
   A solis ortus cardine.

4. The shepherds heard an angel's cry,
   A merye song then sungyn he:
   Why are ye so sore aghast?
   Iam ortus solis cardine.

5. The angels came down with one cry;
   A fair song that night sungyn they
   In the worship of that Child:
   Gloria tibi Domine.

WE USE A slightly modernized version of a carol that dates back over six hundred years, the earliest MS in existence slightly predating Chaucer and written in the Chaucerian dialect then spoken in London. The tune is in the Dorian mode—that is, it can be played on the white keys of the piano, beginning and ending on D. The sixth step, however, is not used.

The Latin lines ending the stanzas have the following meanings: 1. Come, creator Spirit (or Holy Ghost); 2. O Trinity, blessed light; 3. Risen from the quarter of the sun (the east); 4. Now risen in the east; 5. Glory to Thee, O Lord.

The Holly and the Ivy

Traditional English

Traditional English
R.F.

Joyfully

1. The hol-ly and the i-vy, When they are both full grown, Of __ all the trees that are in the wood, The __ hol-ly bears the crown: The

2. The hol-ly bears a blos-som, As white as the lil-y flower, And __ Ma-ry bore sweet Je-sus Christ To __ be our sweet Sav-iour:

3. The holly bears a berry,
   As red as any blood,
   And Mary bore sweet Jesus Christ
   To do poor sinners good:

4. The holly bears a prickle,
   As sharp as any thorn,
   And Mary bore sweet Jesus Christ
   On Christmas Day in the morn:

5. The holly bears a bark,
   As bitter as any gall,
   And Mary bore sweet Jesus Christ
   For to redeem us all:

6. The holly and the ivy,
   When they are both full grown,
   Of all the trees that are in the wood,
   The holly bears the crown:

ris - ing of the sun _____ And the run- ning of the deer, The _____

play-ing of the mer - ry or - gan, Sweet sing-ing in the choir.

THE ASSOCIATION of holly and ivy—especially holly—with wintertime religious festivities antedates Christianity. The Druids so used them in Gaul; the Romans used holly in their Saturnalia on many a December 17. Sexual symbolism usually played a part, the holly being generally regarded as masculine, the ivy as feminine, and the distinction is suggested in this carol. In some rural parts of England, particularly Derbyshire, the superstition still obtains that if rough holly is brought into the house at Christmastime, the husband will be master; if smooth, the wife. There are many carols on the subject, mostly to gay tunes. This one was first recorded by Cecil Sharp about fifty years ago and is found in his *English Folk-Carols*.

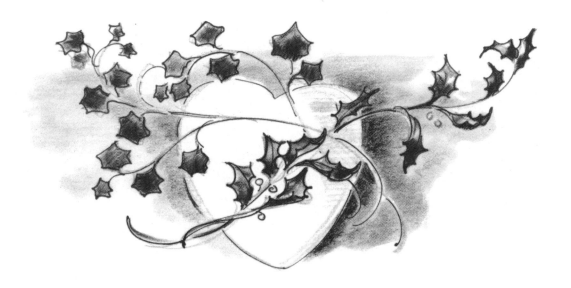

THE ANGEL GABRIEL

Traditional English
Firmly but joyfully

Traditional English
R.F.

1. The An - gel Ga - bri - el from God Was sent to Gal - i - lee, Un -
2. Ma - ry a - non looked him up - on, And said, "Sir, what are ye? I

to a vir - gin fair and free, Whose name was called Ma - ry. And
mar - vel much at these ti - dings Which thou hast brought to me. Mar -

when the An - gel thith - er came, He fell down on his knee, And
ried I am un - to an old man, As the lot fell un - to me; There -

LIKE MANY another old carol in this book, *The Angel Gabriel* seems to modern ears to hover temporarily between the major and the minor, and at last settle for the minor. And like those other carols (see, for example, *God Rest You Merry, Gentlemen*, p. 10), it is neither in major nor in minor, but in one of the old modes, this time the Dorian. Although our key signature is given with one flat, and the melody ends decisively on D, it may be played entirely on the white keys. B-flat and C-sharp are avoided throughout the melody. Yet, after centuries of traffic

with the major and the minor, our ears demand these tones in the harmonization.

The carol was first printed in the 19th century, at which point no one had any guess as to its date of origin. The 15th century would not be a bad one, the place very likely Devonshire. The second stanza commemorates the apocryphal legend that Joseph was chosen to be Mary's husband "by lot," or by a sign from God: of all her suitors, this "old man's" rod miraculously put forth buds.

look-ing up in the vir-gin's face, He said,— "All— hail, Ma-ry": Then
fore, I pray, de-part a-way, For I— stand in doubt of thee": Then

sing we all, both great and small, Now-ell, Now-ell, Now-ell; We

may re-joice to hear the voice Of the An-gel— Ga-bri-el.

3. "Mary," he said, "be not afraid,
   But do believe in me:
   The power of the Holy Ghost
   Shall overshadow thee;
   Thou shalt conceive without any grief,
   As the Lord told unto me;
   God's own dear Son from Heaven shall come,
   And shall be born of thee":
   Refrain:

4. The shepherds heard an angel's cry,
   The which do hear my voice,
   With one accord let's praise the Lord,
   And in our hearts rejoice;
   Like sister and brother, let's love one another
   Whilst we our lives do spend,
   Whilst we have space let's pray for grace,
   And so let my carol end:
   Refrain:

Nuns in Frigid Cells

Henry W. Longfellow (1807–1882)

Traditional
R.F.

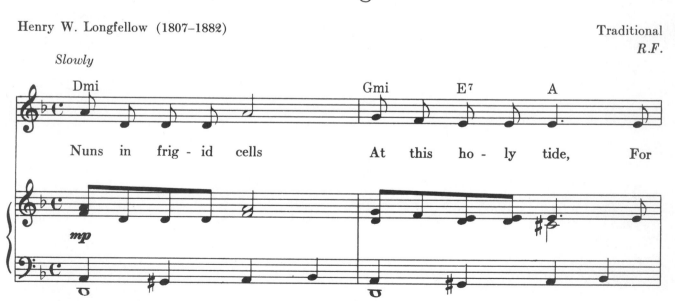

Slowly

Nuns in frig - id cells   At this ho - ly tide,   For

SLY HUMOR is scarcely the attribute one easily associates with Harvard's early professor of modern languages. Yet it is hard to believe that these verses, which come in the middle of a longer poem on Christmas generally very sweet in character, were not intended to evoke smiles. The tune is in the Aeolian mode.

As Joseph Was A-Walking

4. "He neither shall be clothéd in purple nor in pall,
   But in the fair white linen that usen babies all."

5. "He neither shall be rockéd in silver nor in gold,
   But in a wooden cradle that rocks upon the mold."

6. "On the sixth day of January His birthday shall be,
   When the stars and the elements shall tremble with glee."

7. As Joseph was a-walking, thus did the angel sing;
   And Mary's Son at midnight was born to be our King.

THE POEM has a British origin, and there is also an older British tune. But the carol has become so transmuted in its Southern Appalachian version that it takes on the distinctive character of a "white spiritual." This version of the poem was noted down by Richard Chase of Big Stove Gap, Virginia. The sixth stanza puts the physical birth of Jesus on Epiphany—a dating more common in the East than in the New World. The tune, like many white spirituals, uses only the notes of the pentatonic scale.

47

Irish Carol

possibly by Luke Wadding (1588–1657)
Gaily, but without rushing

Traditional Irish
R.F.

1. Christ- mas Day is come; __ let's all pre- pare for __ mirth, Which
2. But why should we re - joice? __ Should we not rath - er __ mourn To

fills the heav'ns and earth __ at this a - maz - ing birth. Through
see the Hope of Na - tions thus in a __ sta - ble born? Where

both the joy - ous an - gels in strife and hur - ry __ fly, With
are His crown and scep - tre, where is His throne sub - lime, Where

glory and ho - san - nas; "All Ho - ly" ___ do they cry, In
is His train ma - jes - tic that should the ___ stars out- shine? Is

heaven the Church tri - um - phant a - dores with all her choirs, The
there no sump - tuous pal - ace nor an - y inn at all To

mil - i - tant on earth ____ with hum - ble faith ad - mires.
lodge His heav'n - ly moth - er but in a filth - y stall?

3. If we would then rejoice, let's cancel the old score,
And purposing amendment, resolve to sin no more—
For mirth can ne'er content us, without a conscience clear;
And thus we'll find true pleasure in all the usual cheer,
In dancing, sporting, rev'ling, with masquerade and drum,
So make our Christmas merry, as Christians doth become.

THE WORDS and the tune were taken down from a singer in county Wexford, Ireland, some thirty or more years ago by Dr. William Henry Grattan Flood, the historian of Irish music. During the 17th century Bishop Luke Wadding used to compose hymns and carols for Irish folk tunes that had previously been sung to profane words. This may well have been one of his efforts, though in the course of three hundred years of folk use both words and tune must have undergone considerable change. Certainly the gay syncopation of the tune and the absence of the fourth step in the scale suggest genuine folk origin.

What Child Is This?

William Chatterton Dix (1837-1898)
With Motion

16th-century English
R.F.

1. What Child is this, _ Who, laid to rest, _ On Ma - ry's lap _ is sleep - ing?Whom
2. Why lies He in _ such mean es - tate Where ox and ass _ are feed - ing? Good
3. So bring Him in - cense, gold, and myrrh, Come,peas-ant,king _ to own Him; The

an - gels greet _ with an - thems sweet, _ While shep - herds watch _ are keep - ing?
Chris - tian,fear: _ for sin - ners here _ The si - lent Word _ is plead - ing.
King of kings _ sal - va - tion brings, _ Let lov - ing hearts _ en - throne him.

REFRAIN:

This, this _ is Christ the King, _ Whom shep - herds guard _ and an - gels sing:

This,   this _ is Christ the King, _ The Babe, _ the Son _ of Ma - ry.

GREENSLEEVES is the name of the tune—one of the most popular folk melodies that ever came out of England, and one that has been put to the most multifarious uses. The first known reference to it came in September, 1580, when a license for printing it was issued by the Stationers' Company to Richard Jones. It was then described as "a new Northern Dittye of the Lady Greene Sleeves." This was probably some version of the now familiar old torch song beginning:

> Alas, my lover, you do me wrong
> To treat me so discourteously.

Ten days later, it was licensed again as "Green Sleves, moralised to the Scripture, declaring the manifold benefites and blessings of God bestowed on sinful man." Before the century was out, it had been licensed several more times, and a year or two later Falstaff was referring to it twice in each performance of *The Merry Wives of Windsor.* (For the curious: the references come in Acts II and V). Several generations after that, the

Cavaliers were using the tune as a party song during the Civil War, and Pepys referred to it, in his *Diary* entry of April 23, 1660, under the name of "The Blacksmith." More recently, in waltz form, it has been the theme tune of a midnight program of serious music broadcast by radio station WNBC. It has also been popular, slightly jazzed up, in night clubs and on jukeboxes.

In England today it is used alternatively with the "Lady Greene Sleeves" words, with a 17th-century set of verses celebrating (rather pathetically) the New Year, and with the present words about the Christ Child. These words were written the reign of Victoria, by a scholarly hymn writer and company executive of Bristol, England.

In all these uses, there have, naturally, been so in the melody itself. The principal differences hav fifth note of the tune is often sung a half tone third note of the refrain a half tone lower.

The Three Ships

Alfred Noyes (1880–   )   Colin Taylor (1881–   )

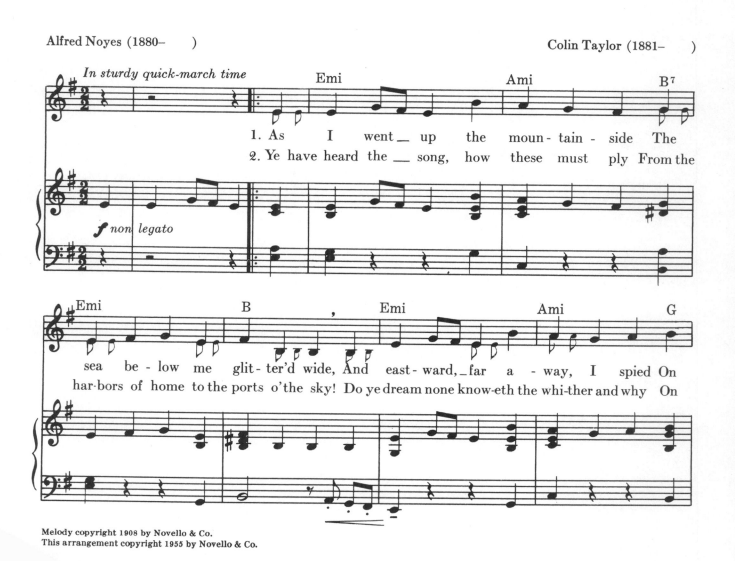

In sturdy quick-march time

1. As I went up the moun-tain-side The
2. Ye have heard the song, how these must ply From the

f non legato

sea be-low me glit-ter'd wide, And east-ward, far a-way, I spied On
har-bors of home to the ports o'the sky! Do ye dream none know-eth the whi-ther and why On

3. Yet as I live, I never knew
That ever a song could ring so true,
Till I saw them break through a haze of blue
On Christmas Day, on Christmas Day;
And the marvelous ancient flags they flew
On Christmas Day in the morning!

4. From the heights above the belfried town
I saw that the sails were patched and brown,
But the flags were aflame with a great renown
On Christmas Day, on Christmas Day,
And on every mast was a golden crown
On Christmas Day in the morning.

5. The sun and the wind they told me there
How goodly a load the three ships bear,
For the first is gold and the second is myrrh,
On Christmas Day, on Christmas Day;
And the third is frankincense most rare,
On Christmas Day in the morning.

6. They have mixed their shrouds with the golden sky,
They have faded away where the last dreams die.
Ah yet, will ye watch, when the mist lifts high
On Christmas Day, on Christmas Day?
Will ye see three ships come sailing by
On Christmas Day in the morning?

NEAR THE TURN of the century, when still in his twenties, the beloved English poet wrote these verses as a Christmas song for the Musical Society of Eton College. They commemorate an old legend connected with the visit of the three Wise Men.

Both words and music effectively assume the guise of an ancient English carol. Yet never did a genuine folk song use a single rhyme per stanza with a technique so immaculate; nor are there many tunes—modal or more modern—that lead so skillfully up to and away from its climax.

Colin Taylor, an English organist and composer who settled in South Africa, originally published his setting for mixed chorus and orchestra. Almost half a century later, he graciously composed the present accompaniment especially for this volume.

RISE UP, SHEPHERD, AND FOLLOW!

Negro Spiritual

Negro Spiritual
R.F.

There's a star in the East on Christ - mas morn;

fol - low! *Rise up, shep-herd, and fol-low!* ___ Fol - low the star of

Beth - le - hem; ___ *Rise up, shep-herd, and fol - low!* ___

TO GET the leader-and-chorus effect most simply, it is suggested that a single voice sing every other line, and that the group come in only on the words *Rise up, shepherd, and follow!*

That is why we have printed this line in italics throughout.

Carols from Foreign Parts

Silent Night

Stille Nacht

Joseph Mohr (1792–1848)

Franz Xavier Gruber (1787–1863)

H.W.S.

1. Si - lent night, ho - ly night! All is calm, all is bright Round yon Vir - gin

1. Stil - le Nacht, hei - li - ge Nacht! Al - les schläft, ein - sam wacht Nur das trau - te hoch-

Moth - er and Child. / Ho - ly In - fant so / ten - der and mild,
hei - li - ge Paar, / Hol - der Kna - be mit / lok - ki - gem Haar.

Sleep in heav - en - ly peace, ___ / Sleep in heav - en - ly peace.
Schlaf in himm - li - scher Ruh, ___ / Schlaf in himm - li - scher Ruh!

omit for last stanza

2. Silent night, holy night!
   Shepherds quake at the sight,
   Glories stream from heaven afar,
   Heav'nly hosts sing alleluia;
   Christ the Saviour is born!
   Christ the Saviour is born!

3. Silent night, holy night!
   Wondrous star, lend thy light!
   With the angels let us sing
   Alleluia to our King!
   Christ the Saviour is here,
   Jesus the Saviour is here!

2. *Stille Nacht, heilige Nacht!*
   Hirten erst kund gemacht;
   Durch der Engel Halleluja
   Tönt es laut von fern und nah:
   Christ, der Retter, ist da!
   Christ, der Retter, ist da!

3. *Stille Nacht, heilige Nacht!*
   Gottes Sohn, O wie lacht
   Lieb' aus deinem göttlichen Mund,
   Da uns schlägt die rettende Stund',
   Christ in deiner Geburt,
   Christ in deiner Geburt!

ON CHRISTMAS EVE, 1818, in the little church of the Austrian village of Oberndorf, the organ was out of order. The 26-year-old assistant pastor, Joseph Mohr, thought something special should be done to make up for the mishap, and he wrote the words of *Silent Night*. He gave them to his friend the village schoolmaster, Franz Gruber, who customarily doubled as church organist. Gruber returned the verses, set for two solo voices, chorus, and guitar on the same day; and that evening the most widely loved Christmas song in the world was heard for the first time.

One of those who heard it was the man engaged to put the organ back into working order. When he went home to the Zillerthal, he took a copy with him and gave it to the Strasser sisters, a touring troupe that specialized in Tyrolean songs. They made it popular everywhere they went. Apparently they did not mention the composer's name; perhaps they never knew it. At any rate, the notion was spread that it was the composition of Michael Haydn, Joseph's younger brother and teacher of Karl Maria von Weber. A governmental investigating committee from Berlin discovered the truth in 1854, when Gruber's son, himself an organist by that time, produced a copy of the original manuscript. The melody was unmistakable, though changes had crept in—changes that the world seems to have decided were improvements. Haydn still is often credited with the melody. One can restore the credit to the real composer, but retain the improvement time has made on his original tune.

Unto Us a Boy Was Born

Old German and Latin sources

paraphrased by Willys Peck Kent

Piae Cantiones, 1582

H.W.S.

1. Un - to us a boy was born; Wel - come, lit - tle stran - ger!

In a barn he found a home, His cra - dle was a man - - - - - - ger.

2. Cattle lowed while angels sang
   On this blest occasion;
   Oxen fell upon their knees
   To show their adoration.

3. When the boy was twelve years old,
   To the temple going,
   There he sat with doctors wise,
   To them the truth was showing.

4. Sick folk came to him for help,
   Rich men left their revels.
   Comfort to the poor he brought
   And cast out many devils.

5. Joy he brought to all the world,
   Chance that comes to few here,
   And today he lives again
   To wish us Happy New Year.

THE OLDEST known version of these words occur in a Latin MS, probably of the 15th century, found in Germany. The oldest German version is a printed one, from Mainz, dated 1544. This begins: *Uns ist geborn ein Kindelein.* There are a number of later versions, too; and, of course, many English translations. Mr. Kent's paraphrase features the medieval idea of animals kneeling at the crib in adoration.

I have held the last note of the melody two full measures longer, in the accompaniment, than do other modern transcriptions of the original version of the tune, thus filling out the normal four-bar phrase pattern.

Whence Comes This Rush of Wings

Traditional French

Traditional French
R.F.

Quietly, wonderingly

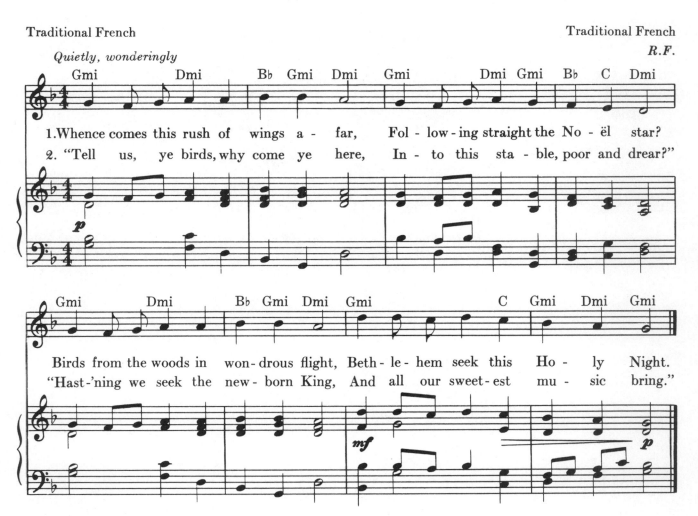

1. Whence comes this rush of wings a - far, Fol - low - ing straight the No - ël star?
2. "Tell us, ye birds, why come ye here, In - to this sta - ble, poor and drear?"

Birds from the woods in won - drous flight, Beth - le - hem seek this Ho - ly Night.
"Hast-'ning we seek the new - born King, And all our sweet - est mu - sic bring."

3. Hark how the Greenfinch bears his part,
Philomel, too, with tender heart,
Chants from her leafy dark retreat
Re, mi, fa, sol, in accents sweet.

4. Angels and shepherds, birds of the sky,
Come where the Son of God doth lie;
Christ on the earth with man doth dwell,
Join in the shout, Noël, Noël.

THE ORIGINS of this old carol seem to lie in the marshy country of Bas Quercy in the southern part of what was once Gascony and is now Basses-Pyrénées, near the Spanish border. The modal tune we sing to it is at least four hundred years old. But the reference in the poem to notes of the scale, which are not to be found in our tune, may indicate that there was once an even older tune, now lost.

Cold Is the Morning

Willys Peck Kent (1877–   )

Czech Folk Tune

R.F.

THE ATTRACTIVE folk tune has had many different sets of words —in French, German, and English as well as Czech. Most of them have to do with Christ in the manger; but as there are already a large number of carols in this collection on that subject, I have borrowed an original poem by Mr. Kent which suggests waifs singing outside one's door early on Christmas morning.

Our arrangement reflects a prevailing characteristic of much Czech folk music in triple time—an accent on the second beat.

Rocking

Traditional Czech
translated by "O.B.C."

Traditional Czech
R.F.

Tenderly

pp

1. Lit - tle Je - sus, sweet - ly __ sleep, do not __ stir;
2. Ma - ry's lit - tle Ba - by, __ sleep, sweet - ly __ sleep,

We will __ lend a __ coat of __ fur, We will rock you, rock you, rock you,
Sleep in __ com - fort, __ slum - ber __ deep; We will rock you, rock you, rock you,

We will rock you, rock you, rock you: See the fur to
We will rock you, rock you, rock you: We will serve you

AMONG the many things that committees do not usually under-
take successfully is the writing of verses. A rare exception is
this translation; the initials "O.B.C." at the head of the page
stand for an otherwise anonymous group of contributors to the
Oxford Book of Carols, which produced its tiny masterpiece
some thirty years ago. The Czech lines begin, *Hajej, nynjej.*

keep you _ warm, Snug - ly _ round your _ ti - ny _ form.
all we _ can, Dar - ling, _ dar - ling _ lit - tle _ man.

Carol of the Flowers

The Song of the Three Wise Men

Willys Peck Kent (1877–   )

Old French
H.W.S.

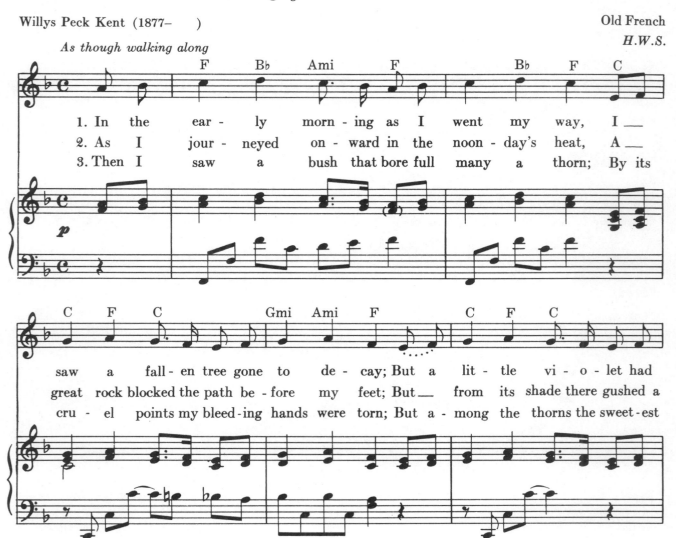

1. In the ear-ly morn-ing as I went my way, I saw a fall-en tree gone to de-cay; But a lit-tle vi-o-let had

2. As I jour-neyed on-ward in the noon-day's heat, A great rock blocked the path be-fore my feet; But from its shade there gushed a

3. Then I saw a bush that bore full many a thorn; By its cru-el points my bleed-ing hands were torn; But a-mong the thorns the sweet-est

found its shade, And— in the cool-ness there its home had made.
cool-ing spring, And it quenched our thirst and made our hearts to sing.
ber-ries grew, And we ate with joy and did our strength re - new:

4. When the night seems dark - est and our hope is gone, In the

East we see the signs of com - ing dawn.

MR. KENT's charming poem is set to a French folk tune that probably dates from the 18th century. It may be sung as a solo throughout. Alternatively, it is suggested that three different singers sing each of the stanzas, the last one beginning with one voice and the others added in the following parts:

When the night seems dark - est and our hope is gone,

In the east we see the signs of com - ing dawn.

Christ Was Born on Christmas Day

Traditional German

Gently, quietly throughout

Traditional German
H.W.S.

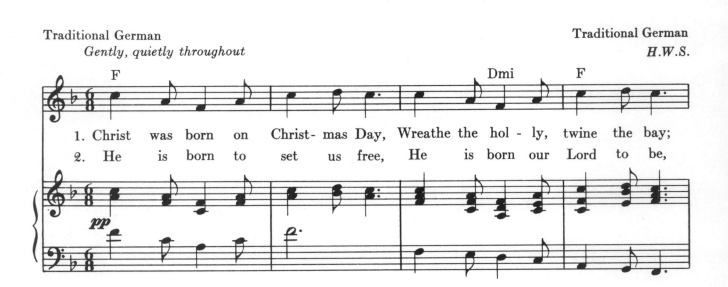

1. Christ was born on Christ-mas Day, Wreathe the hol - ly, twine the bay;
2. He is born to set us free, He is born our Lord to be,

Christ - us na - tus ho - di - e; The Babe, the Son, the
Ex Ma - ri - a Vir - gi - ne, The God, the Lord, by

Ho - ly One of Ma - ry, of Ma - ry.
all a - dored for - ev - er, for - ev - er.

3. Let the bright red berries glow,
   Ev'rywhere in goodly show,
   Christus natus hodie;
   The Babe, the Son, the Holy One of Mary, of Mary.

4. Christian men, rejoice and sing,
   'Tis the birthday of a King,
   Ex Maria Virgine;
   The God, the Lord, by all adored forever, forever.

THIS IS one of the old carols that naïvely mixes the Latin and vernacular, such verses, quite common in medieval popular songs, sacred and profane, being known as macaronic. One version, popular in Germany, comes from a medieval mystery play. Mary begins with the words,

Joseph lieber, Joseph mein,
Hilf mir wiegen mein Kindelein.

There is also an old Latin version beginning, *Resonet in laudibus,* which dates from 1544.

The melody, which has the swing of a lullaby, dates back at least to the 16th century. It has been adapted effectively by two 19th-century German composers as *obbligati* to art songs. Brahms used it thus in one of his songs for alto and viola, Peter Cornelius in one of his Christmas cycle of songs, *Christkind.* Most modern printed versions do not include the repetition of the final measure, as we do.

Hear, O Shepherds
Oj pastiri

Traditional Croatian
Gaily, but not too fast

Traditional Croatian

Hear, O shep-herds, hear while I tell you, Hark to the mir-a-cle that
Oj pa-sti-ri, ču-do____ no-vo, Je-ste li i-kad____

on-ly now be-fell you: On a cra-dle low-ly,
vi-dje-li o-vo: U ja-sli-ci pro-stoj

In a prick-ly stall, Lies the Ba-by ho-ly Who will save us all.
Ro-di-o se bog, Na sla-mi-ci o-štroj Ra-di pu-ka svog,

Lies the Ba-by ho-ly Who will save us all.
Na sla-mi-ci o-štroj Ra-di pu-ka svog.

DEDA MRAZ—that is, Grandpa Frost—is today replacing Santa Claus as the presiding officer of midwinter festivities in Yugoslavia, and the holidays are observed on December 31 and January 1 more often than on the traditional Christmas Day. Nevertheless, the story of the birth of Jesus is still celebrated in carols, and *Oj Pastiri* is one of the most popular of these. It was sent to me by Dr. Louis Goranin of the Yugoslavian consulate in New York.

Dr. Goranin is a musician as well as a diplomat and graciously accompanied the text and a verbatim prose translation with his own harmonization of the tune. All I had to do was to supply a few rhymes.

Midnight, Sleeping Bethlehem

Yang Ching Chin
Not too slowly

Liang Chien Fong
R.F.

1. Mid- night, sleep - ing Beth - le - hem, Stars a- bove are shin - ing_ bright;
2. Mid- night, sleep - ing Beth - le - hem, Can - dles blink-ing from _with - in.
3. Though my soul be lost by my sin, Sin that killed my will _ for _ truth,

Sud - den - ly a shaft light - ens up the sky; Star - tled shep - herds wake in fright.
Wrapped in swad-dling clothes in a man - ger, Come to save the world from sin,
Though I gave my heart up to ev - il, Lost the bless - ing of Thy truth,

Hosts of an - gels sing a song Of the maid - en un - de - filed;
Yes - ter - day He dwelt with God, Now a babe in blank - ets curled,
Thou hast sent a shep - herd here. Could I be a sheep once more,

Dmi⁷   C   Dmi

Sing the birth - day of the Child. Praise the Lord, Al - le - lu - ia,
Bear the suf - fering of this world. Praise the Lord, Al - le - lu - ia,
Thou couldst stay with - in my heart, Though the inn hath closed its door;

F   C   F   Dmi   F

Peace on earth, good will to men. Peace on earth, good will to men.
Peace on earth, good will to men. Peace on earth, good will to men.
Thou couldst stay with - in my heart, Though the inn hath closed its door.

IN 1936 a committee representing six Protestant churches in China produced a Chinese-language hymnal entitled *Hymns of Universal Praise.* An effort was made to include, among the 550 songs, many Christian hymns of Chinese origin; but in the Christmas section, this is the only one with both words and music composed by Orientals. It is composed in the pentatonic scale: that is, like much Oriental music and certain Occidental folk tunes, it may be played entirely on the black keys of our pianos. Mr. Fellner's ingenious arrangement achieves its Orien- tal effect by largely eschewing the strictly Western concept of vertical chords, relying on imitation, and adhering to the penta- tonic scale throughout. Imagine a key signature of six sharps, and the whole piece can be played on the black keys.

Miss Joyce Chang has kindly supplied me with a literal Eng- lish translation of Mr. Yang's poem. I have attempted this ver- sification to fit Mr. Liang's tune, retaining the scheme of rhyming even lines only, which is standard practice in Chinese hymn- writing when the lines are short.

Polish Lullaby
Lulajże Jezuniu

Traditional Polish
translated by **H.W.S.**
Tenderly

Traditional Polish
H.W.S.

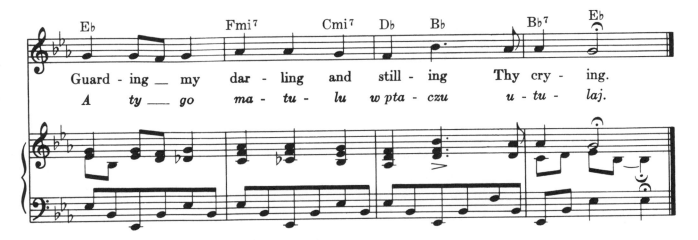

Guard - ing — my dar - ling and still - ing Thy cry - ing.
A ty — go ma - tu - lu w pta - czu u - tu - laj.

2. When Thou awakenest, Jesus, my treasure,
   Raisins and almonds I have for Thy pleasure.

3. High in the heavens a lovely star sees us,
   But like the shining sun, my little Jesus.

2. *Dam ja Ci stodkiego, Jezu, cukierku,*
   Rodzenków, migdałów co mam wpudetku.

3. *Lulajze przyjema oczom Gwiazdeczko,*
   Lulaj najsliczniejsze świata stoneczko.

PIANISTS will recognize this melody as one of the many folk tunes adapted by Chopin. It appears in his *Scherzo in B minor, Opus 20.*

Mrs. Casimir Wierzynski, wife of Chopin's finest biographer, made a literal English prose translation for me, and I have paraphrased it into English verse.

In Dulci Jubilo

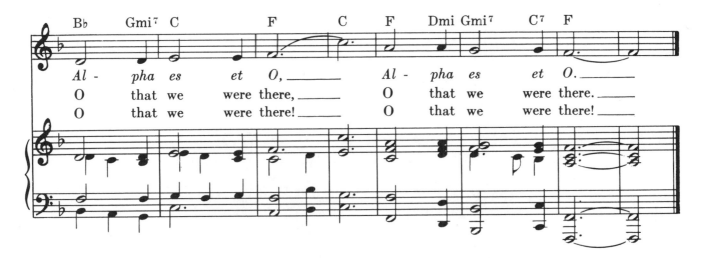

Al - pha es et O, _____ Al - pha es et O. _____
O that we were there, _____ O that we were there. _____
O that we were there! _____ O that we were there! _____

ACCORDING to the charming legend, which I am thoroughly in favor of believing, Henry Suso, the Dominican mystic, heard this carol in a dream one night when angels came to dance for him, singing the gay little waltz tune. Their words, half Latin, half German, began:

In dulci jubilo
Nu singet und seyt fro.

Suso joined in the dance and wrote down the carol when he woke up. But it is no legend that on September 14, 1745, it was sung at the Moravian Mission in what is today Bethlehem, Pennsylvania, in thirteen languages simultaneously, including Bohemian, Dutch, Greek, Latin, Wendish, and Mohawk.

The tune has been revised and harmonized over and over by many. Bach, for example, made a complex harmonization which strikes our ears as ingenious and utterly out of keeping with the simple joy expressed in the words and melody. There have also been, since the beginning of the 18th century, numerous English translations. Ours is that by Robert Lucas de Pearsall. It retains the Latin lines, which the more popular one by John M. Neale (*Good Christian Men, Rejoice*) does not.

Here are literal translations of the Latin phrases: *In dulci jubilo*—in sweet jubilation; *In praesepio*—in a manger; *Matris in gremio*—in the mother's lap; *Alpha es et O*—Thou art the beginning and the end; *O patris caritas, O nati lenitas*—O love of the Father, O gentleness of the Son; *Per nostra crimina*—by our crimes; *Coelorum gaudia*—the joys of Heaven; *Ubi sunt gaudia*—where are the joys? *Nova cantica*—new songs; *In regis curia*—in the court of the King.

Lippai

Traditional Tyrolean
English version by H.W.S.
   Rather coarsely

Traditional Tyrolean
R.F.

1. Lip - pai, — don't — play you're dead! What's — all the row? I
1. Lip - pai, — steh — auf vom Schlaf! "Was — ist denn da?" Mich

can't think — why you stay a - bed. I'm — sleep - ing now.
wun - dert's, — dass d' schla - fen kannst."Ich — schlaf — schon."

Look with me o- ver there, Won- ders are ev-'ry-where;
Geh mit mir auf die Weid, Schau, was für Wun-der geit.

Don't you be left be- hind! What's on your mind?
'S ist so licht wie am Tag. "Was wär das?"

2. Listen, the angels' song!
Can't hear it yet.
Come, take your pipe along.
I'm all set.
They're singing loud and clear
That a new child is here.
What if the Saviour's there?
That would be rare!

3. Now I know we must go!
What's that to me?
An angel told me so.
Personally?
A virgin is somehow
The new child's mother now;
Get up, don't be a toad!
Let's hit the road.

4. That boy is good and gay.
What's his name?
He's lying in the hay.
That's a shame!
I'll ask the mother mild
If I may take the child;
That would rejoice my heart!
Now you're talking smart.

2. *Die Musik währt schon lang.*
"Ich hör nicht."
Trag deine Pfeif auch bei dir!
"Bin schon gericht't."
D'Engel, die singen ob'n:
Es ist ein Kind geborn.
Wenns der Messias wär!
"Das wär rar."

3. *Bethlehem heisst der Ort!*
"Wer hat's gesagt?"
Ich hab's vom Engel g'hört.
"Hast ihn gefragt?"
Ein Jungfrau keusch und rein
Soll seine Mutter sein,
Dort wo der Stern brinnt.
"Geh nur geschwind!"

4. *So schön ist keins geborn*
Wie das Kind!
Dass's auf dem Heu muss lieg'n
Is rechte Sünd!
Ich tu die Mutter fragn
Ob ich's mit mir darf tragn;
Ich hätt die grösste Freud.
"Du redst gescheit."

IF THIS slangy dialogue of the two young shepherds were trans- lated absolutely literally, it would sound startlingly like the speech of Damon Runyon characters. The naïve and artless comedy of the shepherds has a long and quite respectable tradi- tion, going back to the mystery plays of the 15th century.

"Lippai" is very likely a nickname for Leporello, traditionally a bumpkin's name. The tune is as genuinely Tyrolean as the dia- lect: one can fairly hear the leather shorts being slapped as the carolers dance.

Foom, Foom, Foom!

Fum, fum, fum!

Traditional Spanish
translated by H.W.S.
With marked rhythm

Traditional Spanish
R.F.

1. On De-cem-ber twen-ty-five, sing foom, foom, foom!
1.¡Vein-ti-cin-co de di-ciem-bre, fum, fum, fum!

On De-cem-ber twen-ty five, sing foom, foom, foom! He is
¡Vein-ti-cin-co de di-ciem-bre, fum, fum, fum! Na-ci-

born for love of us, The lit-tle God, the ba-by God: Of the
do ha por nues-tro a mor, el Ni-ño Dios, el Ni-ño Dios; hoy de

Vir-gin born a-live This cold De-cem-ber twen-ty-five, Sing foom, foom, foom!
la vir-gen Ma-rí-a en es-ta no-che tan fri-a, ¡Fum, fum, fum!

2. Little birds from out the woods,
   sing foom, foom, foom!
   Little birds from out the woods,
   sing foom, foom, foom!
   Leave the little ones at home,
   Abandon them, abandon them;
   Form a cozy nest to please us
   For the little baby Jesus,
   Foom, foom, foom!

3. Little stars up in the sky,
   sing foom, foom, foom!
   Little stars up in the sky,
   sing foom, foom, foom!
   You may look at Jesus crying
   But yourselves must not be crying;
   Make the dark night glitter lightly,
   Make it twinkle purely, brightly,
   Foom, foom, foom!

2. *¡Pajaritos de los bosques,*
   fum, fum, fum!
   ¡Pajaritos de los bosques,
   fum, fum, fum!
   vuestros hijos de coral
   abandonad, abandonad,
   y formad un muelle nido
   a Jesús recién nacido,
   ¡Fum, fum, fum!

3. *¡Estrellitas de los cielos,*
   fum, fum, fum!
   ¡Estrellitas de los cielos,
   fum, fum, fum!
   que a Jesús mirais llorar
   y no lloráis, y no lloráis,
   alumbrad la noche oscura
   con vuestra luz clara y pura,
   ¡Fum, fum, fum!

THE CAROL is Catalan in origin but has been adopted by all of Spain; so it is given in the Spanish rather than the Catalan language. As much as any tune in this book, it suggests the dance use made of carols, with its vigorous rhythm and the suggestion of strummed guitars in the strongly marked *foom-foom-foom*'s. R. F.'s arrangement adds a hint of castanets.

Oxen and Sheep

Entre le boeuf et l'âne gris

Old French

translated by Willys Peck Kent

Old French
H.W.S.

Quietly, gently

Ox - en and sheep Thy guard - ians mild, Slum - ber,
En - tre le boeuf et l'â - ne gris, Dors, dors,

sleep, Thou lit - tle Child! Sleep, Thou lit - tle Child, An - gels pure and white,
dors le pe - tit Fils! Mil - le an-ges di - vins, Mil - le sér - a - phins

Watch - ing all the night a - bove the slum - b'ring
Vo - lent à l'en - tour de ce grand Dieu d'a -

Dmi	Gmi	Dmi⁷	Gmi	Dmi

Child.   Sleep   on,   sleep   on!
mour.   *Dors,*   *dors,*   *dors,*   *dors!*

MANY MODERN collections attribute this lullaby to François August Gevaert (1828–1908), composer, musicologist, and director of the Brussels Conservatory. What M. Gevaert actually did was to take an old French tune—just how old, no one seems to know, but possibly no more than two hundred years—smooth it out a bit, and make a four-part setting for unaccompanied chorus. Our arrangement follows, in general, Gevaert's melodic and harmonic ideas but adapts them freely for a solo voice. Somehow this seems to be more appropriate for Mary's lullaby than a choral arrangement.

Lo, How a Rose E'er Blooming

Es ist ein' Ros' entsprungen

Old German words
translated by **Theodore Baker**

Old German melody
(*harmonized by* Michael Praetorius)
R.F.

| Bb | F | C | | D | Gmi | | F | Gmi | | F | C | | F |

cold   of   win - ter,   When   half   spent   was ___ the   night.
men   a   Sav - iour,   When   half   spent   was ___ the   night.

1. *Es ist ein' Ros' entsprungen*
   Aus einer Wurzel zart;
   Wie uns die Alten sungen,
   Aus Jesse kam die Art.
   Und hat ein' Blümlein bracht,
   Mitten im kalten Winter,
   Wohl zu der halben Nacht.

2. *Das Röslein das ich meine,*
   Davon Isaias sagt,
   Hat uns gebracht alleine
   Marie, die reine Magd.
   Aus Gottes ew'gem Rat
   Hat sie ein Kind geboren,
   Und bleibt doch reine Magd.

AND THERE *shall come forth a rod out of the stem of Jesse, and a Branch shall grow out of his roots.* So, in the 8th century B.C., Isaiah (11:1) prophesied the birth of Jesus. And a thousand years later, the imaginative medieval mind saw the Branch literally bearing one rose in midwinter; and that rose blooms again each Christmas Eve to celebrate the Birth. "when half spent was the night."

The melody, which dates from the early 16th century, first appeared in print, with the words, at Cologne in 1600; and that remarkable German composer and theoretician Michael Praetorius (1571–1621) published his beautiful harmonization of it in 1609 in a volume entitled *Musae Sioniae.*

The familiar translation is the work of the American musicologist Dr. Theodore Baker.

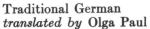

Traditional German
translated by Olga Paul

Traditional German
R.F.

Mary
on
the
Mountain

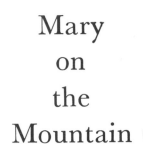

REFRAIN:
Gently

On the moun-tain where breez - es sigh, ____ Was
Auf dem Ber - ge da Weht_ der Wind, ____ Da

heard a di - vine lul - la - by. _____
wiegt die Ma - ri - a ihr Kind. _____

FINE

1. Ma - ri - a was rock-ing her ho - ly Child with
1. Mit ih - rer schloh-en - gel - weis - sen Hand, sie

(Back to refrain)

an - gel white hands_ and fond - ly smiled.
hat auch da - zu_ kein Wie - gen-band.

*Da Capo (Refrain)
after each stanza*

86

Maria auf dem Berge

Mary:

2. "Oh Jo-seph, help me my watch_ to keep, Oh
2. *"Ach Jo-sef, lieb-ster Jo-sef mein, Ach*

(Back to refrain)

help me to lull___ my Child _ to sleep."
hilf mir doch wie-gen mein Kin - de-lein!"

(Back to refrain)

Joseph:

3. "Oh how can I lull_ your Child_ so ho-ly, I
3. *"Wie soll ich dir denn_ dein Kin-de-lein wie-gen? Ich*

(Back to refrain)

hard-ly can bend my poor fin - gers slow-ly."
kann ja kaum sel-ber die Fin-ger-lein bie-gen!"

(Back to refrain)

THIS CHARMING little domestic drama comes from Silesia, in East Prussia, and dates from the Thirty Years' War in the 17th century. In that grim conflict, famine, pestilence, and the ordinary brutalities of war are said to have destroyed three quarters of the men, women, and children of Silesia. There should lie in this fact some lesson about the hardiness of the gentler virtues that could produce so sweet a song in so bitter a time.

It is suggested that one girl sing the first stanza, another the second, and a boy the third, with all three children joining in the refrain as it precedes and follows each solo.

87

THE CHILD JESUS

El Mino Jesus

Traditional Porto Rican
paraphrase by Olga Paul

Traditional Porto Rican
R.F.

Quietly and slowly

1. "Moth-er dear, a Child at our door step Has a beau-ty past com-par-ing; wear-ing." 2. But as soon as He had en-tered, While His

Yet He weeps for He is ___ freez-ing, For you see, no clothes He's mis-tress asked what coun-try Here on

1.
E⁷ · C · F · Ami

warmth He was re - gain - ing,
earth He had

2.
E · Ami · Ami

The—
been reign - ing. 3. "My Fa - ther is from

Dmi · E⁷ · Ami

Heav - en, My Moth - er's ho - ly too;— I've

Ami · Dmi · E⁷ · Ami

come to earth to suf - fer For your sins and you!"

1. "Madre a la puerta hay un niño
Mas hermosa que el sol bello;
Llorando muertó de frío,
Y sim duda riene en cueras."

2. Entra el niño y se colienta y
Después de calentado,
Le pregunta la padrona
De qué tierra es su reinado.

3. "Mi padre es del cielo,
Mi madre también.
Yo barjé a la tierra
Para prodecer!"

THE DRAMATIC FORM, the apocryphal subject, and the primitive language indicate that this is a genuine folk song; and its quiet, almost mystical melody adds to this impression. Yet it is probably not over a hundred years old.

In the Town

15th-century French

paraphrase by Eleanor Farjeon

15th-century French

R.F.

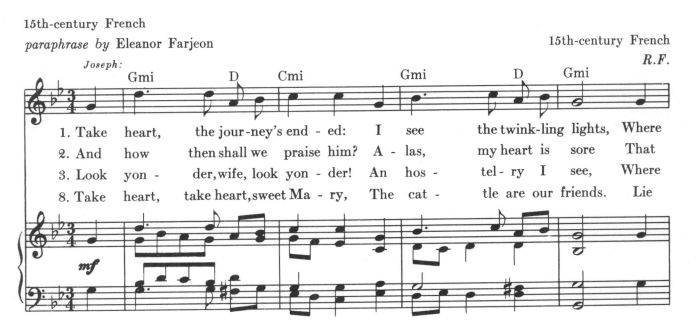

Joseph:

| Gmi | D | Cmi | Gmi | D | Gmi |

1. Take heart, the jour-ney's end - ed: I see the twink-ling lights, Where
2. And how then shall we praise him? A - las, my heart is sore That
3. Look yon - der, wife, look yon - der! An hos - tel- ry I see, Where
8. Take heart, take heart, sweet Ma - ry, The cat - tle are our friends. Lie

mf

THIS HAUNTING little tune, with a range of but six notes, has captured the Gallic taste in so many ways that it has been used variously as an organ prelude, a drinking song, a torch song, and two different Christmas carols. Our carol, which is at least five hundred years old and begins *Nous voici dans la ville,* has been made into a little Christmas play by the poet Eleanor Farjeon. The potential monotony of repeating the same little melody nine times is easily counteracted by distributing and acting out the parts, and by the pianist's taking full advantage of the more aggressive arrangement in the stanzas involving the Host and the Hostess. (Before beginning, it will be well to note the order in which the stanzas follow each other.)

we   shall be be- friend- ed   On   this   the night of nights. Now
we   no gifts can raise him   Who   are   so ver- y   poor. We
trav -   el- ers that wan- der   Will ver-   y wel- come be. The
down,   lie down, sweet Ma - ry, For here   the jour - ney ends. Now

praise   the Lord that led   us   So safe   un - to the town, ___ Where
have   as much as an - y   That on   the earth do live, ___ Al -
house   is tall and state - ly, The door   stands o - pen thus; ___ Yet,
praise   the Lord that found me   This shel - ter in the town, ___ Where

men   will feed and bed us, And   I   can lay me down.
though   we have no pen - ny, We have   our - selves to give.
hus -   band, I fear great - ly That inn   is not for us.
I   with friends a - round me May lay   my bur - den down.

Fine

SLEEP, O HOLY CHILD OF MINE
Dormi, dormi, o bel Bambin

Traditional Italian
translated by Olga Paul

Traditional Italian
R.F.

Tenderly but not too slowly

1. Sleep, O ho-ly Child of mine, King di-vine, King di-vine. Let my lit-tle In-fant slum-ber. King di-vine, King di-vine, Let my lit-tle In-fant slum-ber.

1. Dor-mi, dor-mi, o bel Bam-bin, Rè di-vin, Rè di-vin. Fa la nan-na, o fan-to-li-no. Rè di-vin, Rè di-vin. Fa la nan-na, o fan-to-li-no.

2. Precious love, why do You weep?
Can't You sleep? can't You sleep?
Let my precious Babe now slumber,
Wondrous fair, wondrous fair,
Let my precious Babe now slumber.
Refrain:

2. *Perchè piangi, o mio tresor?*
Dolce amor, dolce amor!
Fa la nanna, a caro figlio,
Tanto bel, tanto bel,
Fa la nanna, o caro figlio.
Refrain:

JUST HOW the holy Child could be expected to sleep to so many gay *fa-la-la*'s is perhaps unclear. But the carol combines the tenderness and high spirits of the season that all children share. The pattern and spirit of the second half is used by Gian-Carlo Menotti with great effect for the carol in *Amahl and the Night Visitors.* Unfortunately, his publishers would not permit me to include it in this collection.

La la la la la la la la la, La la la la la la la la,

Fa la la, la la la, fa la la, la la la, Fa la la, fa la la, fa la la, la.

MARIA WANDERED THROUGH A WOOD

Maria durch ein' Dornwald ging

Old German
translated by H.W.S.

Old German
R.F.

1. Maria wandered through a wood, Kyrie eleison. Through a barren wood of barren thorn That for seven years no bloom had born, Jesus and Maria.

2. What did she lightly carry there? Kyrie eleison. A Child beneath her heart she bare; Maria bare it lightly there. Jesus and Maria.

3. And as the Child was lightly borne, Kyrie eleison. Even as the Child was lightly borne, Bright roses shone among the thorn. Jesus and Maria.

1. *Maria durch ein' Dornwald ging,*
   Kyrie eleison.
   Maria durch ein' Dornwald ging,
   Der hat in sieb'n Jahr'n kein Laub getrag'n.
   Jesus und Maria.

2. *Was trug Maria unter ihrem Herzen?*
   Kyrie eleison.
   Ein kleines Kindlein ohne Schmerzen,
   Das trug Maria unter ihrem Herzen.
   Jesus und Maria.

3. *Da hab'n die Dornen Rosen getrag'n.*
   Kyrie eleison.
   Als das Kindlein durch den Wald getrag'n,
   Da hab'n die Dornen Rosen getrag'n.
   Jesus und Maria.

THE EARLIEST KNOWN reference to this carol dates it no later than the close of the 16th century. However, the simple and dramatic use of the rose-miracle legend, the casual inclusion of the *Kyrie eleison,* and the absence from the melody of the seventh note of the scale all combine to suggest an origin at least a hundred years earlier.

In my translation I have retained the German form for the name of the Virgin. Anyone who wishes to substitute the English "Mary" can simply prefix the first line with the word "As" and give two notes to the first syllable of "Jesus" in the last line.

Bring a Torch, Jeannette, Isabella

Un Flambeau, Jeannette, Isabelle

Traditional French
translated by Edward Cuthbert Nunn
Lively

Traditional French
R.F.

1. Bring a torch,___ Jean-nette, Is-a-bel - la! Bring a torch, to the cra - dle run! It is Je - sus, good folk of the vil - lage;

1. Un flam - beau,___ Jean-nette, Is-a-bel - le, Un flam-beau,___ cou - rons au ber - ceau! C'est Jé - sus, bon - nes gens du ha - meau,___

2. It is wrong when the Child is sleeping,
   It is wrong to talk so loud;
   Silence, all, as you gather around,
   Lest your noise should waken Jesus:
   Hush! hush! see how fast He slumbers;
   Hush! hush! see how fast He sleeps!

3. Softly to the little stable,
   Softly for a moment come;
   Look and see how charming is Jesus,
   How He is white, His cheeks are rosy!
   Hush! hush! see how the Child is sleeping;
   Hush! hush! see how He smiles in dreams.

2. *C'est un tort quand l'Enfant sommeille,*
   C'est un tort de crier si fort.
   Taisez-vous, l'un et l'autre, d'abord!
   Au moindre bruit, Jésus s'éveille,
   Chut! chut! chut!
   Il dort à merveille,
   Chut! chut! chut! voyez comme Il dort!

3. *Doucement, dans l'étable close,*
   Doucement, venez un moment!
   Approchez, que Jésus est charmant!
   Comme Il est blanc, comme Il est rose!
   Do! do! do! que l'Enfant répose!
   Do! do! do! qu'Il rit en dormant!

OUR HEADING conservatively labels the source of both words and tune "traditional," but a good guess as to the origin of both is 17th-century Provence, and some give credit to Nicholas Saboly (1614–1675). The author of the graceful translation used in all English-speaking countries at least is known—though most books do not credit him, either. He was the British organist and composer Edward Cuthbert Nunn (1868–1914).

Acting out a scene beside the cradle of Jesus, as suggested by this carol, is a custom that goes back even farther than the 17th century and was popular, especially on the European continent, in the Middle Ages. And celebrating winter religious festivals with the carrying of torches is still older. Ancient Jews did it as part of the Festival of Lights, or Hanukkah. Mr. Busoni's picture quite properly suggests 17th-century France.

The Carol of the Bagpipers

Canzone d'i Zampognari

Traditional Sicilian
translated by H.W.S.

Traditional Sicilian
R.F.

Serenely

And when the Child was born___ At Beth - le - hem, where He
Quan - no na - sce - te Nin - no a Bet - te - lem -

lay,_____ All through the night It seemed as bright___ As___
e, _____ E - ra___ not - te e pa - - - re - a

though it were mid- day. Nev - er so bright - ly, Beau - ti - fully,
mie - zo juor - no. Ma - je le stel - le, lu - ste - re e

IN THE 18TH CENTURY—and probably much earlier—bagpipers from the neighboring mountains visited Naples during the Christmas season to serenade private homes (see note on *Canon of the Mimes*, p. 229) and statues of the Virgin Mary. It is quite possible, as many have conjectured, that Handel heard the bag-pipers singing this tune during the Christmas season of 1708 when he was in Naples, for it bears a marked resemblance to the opening of *He Shall Feed His Flock* (see p. 201). If so, the tune must have impressed him deeply, for *Messiah* was composed thirty-four years later.

Angels We Have Heard on High
Les Anges dans nos campagnes

Traditional French
Swiftly, joyously

Traditional French
H.W.S.

An - gels we have heard on high,_ Sweet - ly sing - ing o'er the plains,
Les an - ges dans nos cam-pa-gnes Ont en - ton - né l'hymne des cieux;

And the _ moun-tains _ in re - ply. Ech - o - ing their _ joy - ous strains.
Et l'é - cho de nos mon-ta-gnes Re - dit _ ce chant _ mé - lo-dieux:

2. Shepherds, why this jubilee?
   Why your joyous strains prolong?
   What the gladsome tidings be
   Which inspire your heav'nly song?
   Gloria in excelsis Deo,
   Gloria in excelsis Deo.

3. Come to Bethlehem and see
   Him whose birth the angels sing;
   Come, adore on bended knee,
   Christ the Lord, the newborn King.
   Gloria in excelsis Deo,
   Gloria in excelsis Deo.

VARIOUS delightful stories are told about this carol. For instance, Pope Telesphorus in the 2nd century is said to have ordered it sung at midnight mass every Christmas Eve. If so, it must have been a different Gloria, for neither text nor tune is in a style that could be much earlier than the 18th century, the probable time of its anonymous origin in France, or possibly Quebec.

The refrain lends itself so easily to contrapuntal effects that practically every editor of Christmas carols has been tempted to play around with them in some fresh way. I have succumbed to the same temptation, trying to suggest a singing group growing in numbers as the carol goes on.

The tune is often sung to the hymn by James Montgomery, *Angels, from the Realms of Glory* (see p.144).

THE MARCH OF THE KINGS

La Marche des rois

Old French
English version by H.W.S.
March time

Old French
R.F.

At dawn of day, I met them on the way — The three great mon-archs and a
De grand ma- tin J'ai ren-con-tré le train De trois grands rois qui al-laient

host of war- riors, Yes, on that day, I met them on the way, The
en voy - a - ge, De grand ma- tin J'ai ren-con-tré le train De

three great mon-archs with a brave dis - play. All decked in gold Were the
trois grands rois des-sus le grand che - min. Tout char-gés d'or Les sui-

war - riors bold, The no - ble knights and the guard-ians of the trea - sure, Their
vaient d'a - bord De grands guer - riers et les gar - des du tré - sor, Tout

shields and buck-lers were shin-ing bright, And pen-nons glist-ened in the morn-ing light.
char - gés d'or les sui - vaient d'a-bord De grand guer - riers a - vec leurs bou - cli - ers.

WORDS AND TUNE have been known some seven hundred years in Provence, where the carol is also called *Marche de Turenne.* Our version of the tune is based on Georges Bizet's. He used it as one of the twenty-seven pieces of incidental music he com- posed for a performance of Alphonse Daudet's *L'Arlésienne,* a tragedy that takes place on Christmas Eve. With the second voice starting half a measure after the first, one half of the tune can effectively be sung as a canon.

WHILE JESUS SLEEPS

L'Enfant Jésus s'endòrt

Old French

translated by H.W.S.

Old French

arranged by Franz Liszt

108

AT THE AGE of sixty-four, Liszt composed a set of a dozen pieces mostly of modest technical requirements (*zumeist leichterer Spielart,* he labeled them) under the title of *Christmas Tree.* When they were published six years later, they bore a dedication to his granddaughter, Daniela von Bülow. Fräulein Daniela was the daughter of Frau Richard Wagner, Cosima Liszt having supplied her father with two distinguished sons-in-law by that time.

Our piece is the first of the set and bears the title "An Old

Christmas Carol." With the exception of the vocal line and its literal English translation, it is given here as Liszt published it. Our book is intended primarily for the singers in the family, but there is no harm in letting the pianist show off a little bit. Of course, what Liszt regarded as "easy" included the playing of left-hand octaves at any speed under *presto.* The beginner will find things manageable enough if he plays the octaves in single notes (preferably the lower ones)—especially those eighth-note octaves beginning on the third page.

In a Manger

Rutherford Kingsley

pseud. for Carl Engel (1883–1944)

Traditional Russian

harmonized by Michael Mikhailovich Ippolitov-Ivanov (1859–1935)

H.W.S.

Not too slowly

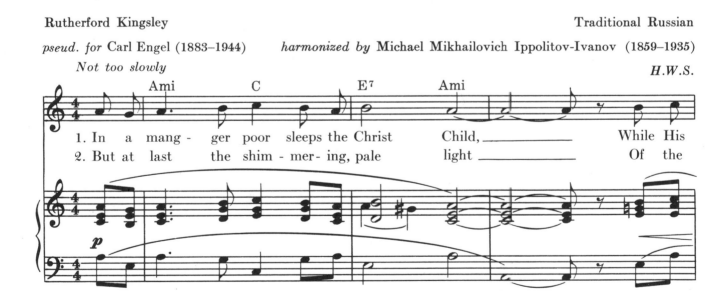

1. In a mang - ger poor sleeps the Christ Child,_____ While His
2. But at last the shim - mer- ing, pale light _____ Of the

THE RHYTHMICAL realization of the old Russian tune as well as the harmonies are based on Ippolitov-Ivanov's composition for mixed choir. It is suggested that the second time through the piano part be played one octave lower, *pianissimo,* as though a male choir were chanting in the next room.

Christmas Hymns and Chorales

CHRISTIANS, AWAKE

John Byrom (1692–1763)

John Wainwright (ca. 1723–1768)

R.F.

1. Chris-tians, a-wake, sa-lute the hap-py morn, Where-on the Sav-iour of the world was born; Rise to a-dore the mys-ter-y of love,

2. Then to the watch-ful shep-herds it was told, Who heard the an-gel-ic her-ald's voice: "Be-hold, I bring good tid-ings of a Sav-iour's birth

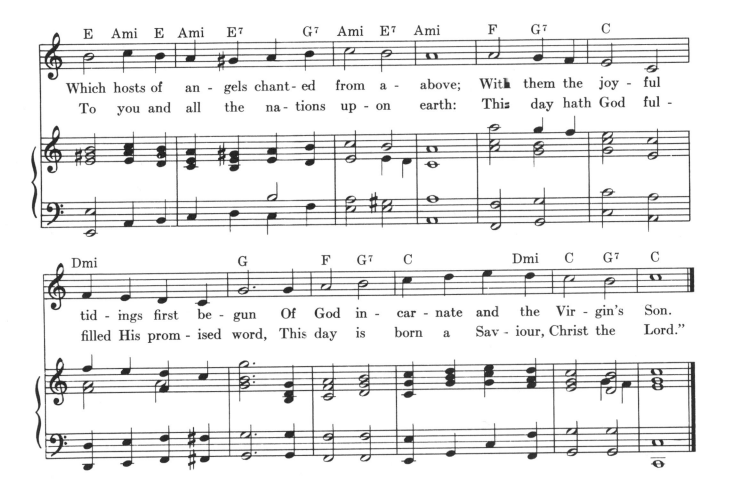

3. He spake, and straightway the celestial choir
   In hymns of joy, unknown before, conspire;
   The praises of redeeming love they sang,
   And heav'ns whole orb with alleluias rang;
   God's highest glory was their anthem still,
   Peace upon earth, and unto men good will.

4. To Bethlehem straight the happy shepherds ran,
   To see the wonder God had wrought for man;
   And found, with Joseph and the blessed Maid,
   Her Son, the Saviour, in a manger laid;
   Amazed, the wondrous story they proclaim,
   The earliest heralds of the Saviour's name.

5. Let us, like these good shepherds, then employ
   Our grateful voices to proclaim the joy;
   Trace we the Babe, who hath retrieved our loss,
   From His poor manger to His bitter cross:
   Treading His steps, assisted by His grace,
   Till man's first heav'nly state again takes place.

6. Then may we hope, the angelic thrones among,
   To sing, redeemed, a glad triumphal song;
   He, that was born upon this joyful day,
   Around us all His glory shall display;
   Saved by His love, incessant we shall sing.
   Of angels and of angelmen the King.

THIS POEM was the author's cheerful Christmas greeting to his daughter Dolly on the morning of December 25, 1749. His friend the organist John Wainwright set it to music, and the following Christmas morning serenaded the Byroms with it, having brought along "the singing men and boys" for the occasion. So it is recorded in Byrom's diary. Byrom was a qualified physician (but didn't practise), a graceful writer (he contributed to *The Spectator*), and the inventor of a system of shorthand which, by act of Parliament, no one else was allowed to teach for twenty-one years. Then he died. Among his shorthand pupils were the Wesleys, whose religious meetings he attended; but he ended his days as a Quaker.

Hush, My Dear, Lie Still and Slumber

Isaac Watts (1674–1748)

J. S. Bach (1685–1750)

H.W.S.

Quietly, gently

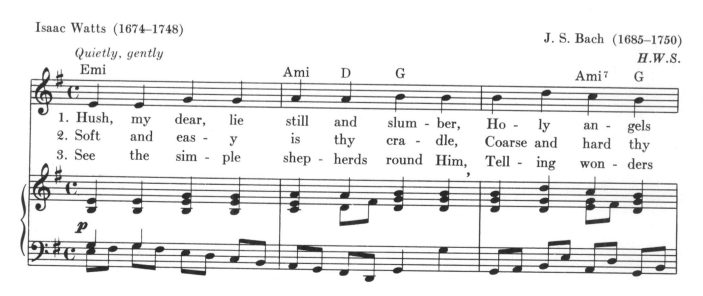

1. Hush, my dear, lie still and slumber, Ho - ly an - gels
2. Soft and eas - y is thy cra - dle, Coarse and hard thy
3. See the sim - ple shep - herds round Him, Tell - ing won - ders

ISAAC WATTS, schoolmaster, preacher, logician, poet, is remembered today chiefly as the great humanizer among hymn writers. His six hundred hymns (among them *O God, Our Help in Ages Past*, *When I Survey the Wondrous Cross*, and *Joy to the World* —see p. 146) earned him a place in Westminster Abbey and in the hearts of all hymn-lovers. He was the first to write children's hymns which are still sung, and he was the author of such familiar verses as *How Doth the Busy Little Bee* and

Let dogs delight to bark and bite,
For God hath made them so.

Hush, My Dear appeared in 1715 in a volume entitled *Divine Songs Attempted in Every Language for the Use of Children*, written for three of his pupils, daughters of his patron, Sir Thomas Abney. Our setting (and the poem has had a number of settings, though none more beautiful) is taken from a cantata, now lost, by the poet's greatest musical contemporary.

Wake, Awake, for Night Is Flying

Wachet auf

Philipp Nicolai (1556–1608)

Majestically

Philipp Nicolai
harmonized by J. S. Bach
H.W.S.

1. Wake, a- wake, for night is fly - ing: The watch - men on __ the
Mid-night's sol- emn hour is toll - ing, His char - iot wheels __ are

heights are cry - ing, A - wake, Je - ru - sa - lem, __ a - rise!
near - er roll - ing, He comes; pre - pare, ye vir - gins wise.

Rise up, with will - ing feet Go forth, the Bride-groom meet! Al - le - lu - ia!

Bear through the night your well-trimm'd light, Speed forth to join the mar-riage rite.

2. Zion hears the watchmen singing,
   Her heart with deep delight is springing,
   She wakes, she rises from her gloom:
   Forth her Bridegroom comes, all glorious,
   In grace arrayed, by truth victorious;
   Her Star is risen, her Light is come!
   All hail, Incarnate Lord,
   Our crown, and our reward!
   Alleluia!
   We haste along, in pomp of song,
   And gladsome join the marriage throng.

3. Lamb of God, the heav'ns adore Thee,
   And men and angels sing before Thee,
   With harp and cymbal's clearest tone.
   By the pearly gates in wonder
   We stand, and swell the voice of thunder
   That echoes round Thy dazzling throne.
   No vision ever brought,
   No ear hath ever caught,
   Such bliss and joy:
   We raise the song, we swell the throng,
   To praise Thee ages all along.

Wachet auf, ruft uns die Stimme
Der Wächter sehr hoch auf der Zinnen,
Wach auf, du Stadt Jerusalem!
Mitternacht heisst diese Stunde,
Sie rufen uns mit hellem Munde,
Wo seid ihr klugen Jungfrauen?
Wohl auf! der Bräutgam kommt,
Steht auf, die Lampen nimmt.
Halleluia!
Macht euch bereit zu der Hochzeit,
Ihr müsset ihm entgegen gehn.

DURING the plague of 1597 at Unna, in Westphalia, 1300 of Pastor Nicolai's parishioners were carried off. The cantankerous but kindly Lutheran helped bury many of them, consoled the bereaved, composed hymns (including, apparently, this one), and kept a spiritual diary. "Day by day," he tells us, "I wrote out my meditations, found myself, thank God! wonderfully well, comforted in heart, joyful in spirit, and truly content." The words and the melody of this magnificent hymn truly affirm the deeply religious joy and confidence of the stern and solid Dutchman.

About a century later another great Lutheran, Johann Sebas-

tian Bach, used Nicolai's words and tune (adding only some passing notes) as the firm foundation of one of his great choral works—*Wachet Auf*, Cantata No. 140. The present harmonization is taken from the final chorale of that work. The translation is largely the work of Catherine Winkworth.

Based on passages from Isaiah and Revelations and on the parable of the Wise and Foolish Virgins, the hymn is not, strictly speaking, a Christmas song, though it is often found in the Christmas section of hymnals, probably on the idea suggested in the opening lines.

O Thou Joyful Day

O sanctissima

Anonymous Latin verses

Italian
R.F.

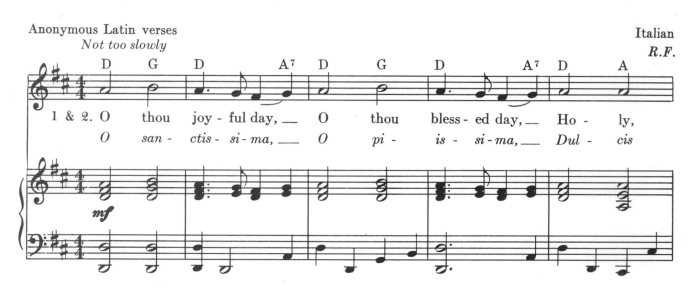

Not too slowly

1 & 2. O thou joy-ful day, ___ O thou bless-ed day, ___ Ho- ly,

O san - ctis-si-ma, ___ O pi - is - si-ma, ___ Dul - cis

peace - ful _ Christ - mas - tide.

Vir _ go Ma - ri - a.

1. Earth's _ hopes a - wak - en,
2. King _____ of _____ glo - ry,

Ma - ter a - ma - ta,

Christ _ life hath tak - en.

We _ bow be - fore _ Thee,

in - te - me - ra - ta,

Laud _ Him, O laud _ Him on ev - 'ry side.

O - ra, _____ o - ra pro no - bis.

THIS TUNE, which has been adapted for a number of hymns, was first printed in several different collections in the late 18th century on both sides of the Atlantic—in the United States and England. The Latin text was used. Meantime, the German poet Johann Gottfried Herder was enjoying a trip to Italy, and some years later, with the same tune, published a German translation. All the early collectors implied an Italian origin, usually Sicilian, sometimes more specifically with the title *Sicilian Mariner's*

Prayer. Yet there is no early Italian publication of the melody; and it is perfectly possible that it comes from one of the hundreds of operas composed and performed at that period but never published.

The Latin verses are a fairly conventional 16th-century prayer to the Virgin. The English-language version adapts it for Christmas—and somehow the melody seems to be especially well suited for the emotion of quiet, almost breathless, wonder.

IT CAME UPON A MIDNIGHT CLEAR

Edmund H. Sears (1810–1876)
Flowing but not too fast

Richard S. Willis (1819–1900)
R.F.

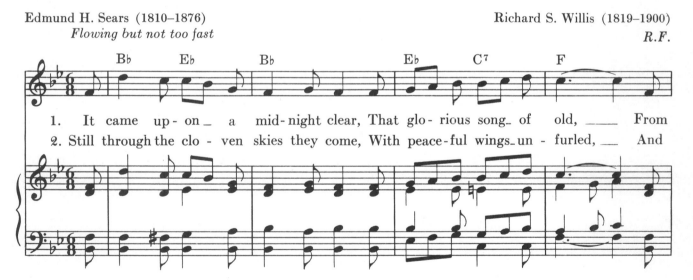

1. It came up-on— a mid-night clear, That glo-rious song— of old, ____ From
2. Still through the clo-ven skies they come, With peace-ful wings— un-furled, ___ And

3. O ye, beneath life's crushing load,
   Whose forms are bending low,
   Who toil along the climbing way,
   With painful steps and slow,
   Look now, for glad and golden hours
   Come swiftly on the wing:
   O rest beside the weary road,
   And hear the angels sing!

4. For lo! the days are hast'ning on,
   By prophets seen of old,
   When with the ever circling years,
   Shall come the time foretold,
   When the new heav'n and earth shall own
   The Prince of Peace their King,
   And the whole world send back the song
   Which now the angels sing.

THE AUTHOR of this carol was a graduate of the Harvard Divinity School, its composer a Yale man. They probably never met. Dr. Sears, a devout and original thinker, was one of the first preachers to insist that "Peace on the earth, good will to men" was one of the greatest messages of the Lord. The verses were first published in the *Christian Register* in 1850, and the editor of that journal, himself a clergyman, later wrote: "I always feel that, however poor my Christmas sermon may be, the reading and singing of this hymn are enough to make up for all deficiencies."

After studying music in Germany, where Mendelssohn was one of his teachers, Willis returned to the United States and combined composing with musical journalism. During one period he acted as critic for the New York *Tribune*. It was while he was a vestryman at the Little Church Around the Corner in New York that he composed the tune under the title of CHRISTMAS CAROL. It is frequently used for the carol *While Shepherds Watched Their Flocks by Night*. The verses Willis had in mind when he first wrote the tune, however, began: "See Israel's gentle shepherd stand." It appeared the same year as Sears's words, but it was some time before the two were joined to make one of the most popular carols in all English-speaking countries.

Break Forth, O Beauteous Heavenly Light

Brich an, du schönes Morgenlicht

Johann Rist (1607-1667)

Johann Schop (*d. ca.*1664)
adapted by J. S. Bach
H.W.S.

Slowly

Break forth, O beaut-eous heaven-ly light, And ush- er in the morn- ing; Ye
Brich an, du schö - nes Mor-gen-licht, Und lass den Him- mel ta - gen; Du

shep- herds, shrink not with af- fright, But hear the an- gel's warn- ing. This
Hir - ten- volk er -stau - ne nicht, Weil dir die En- gel sa - gen, Dass

124

child, now weak in in - fan - cy,   Our con - fi - dence and joy shall be, The
die - ses schwa - che Knä - be - lein   Soll un - ser Trost and Freu - de sein, Da-

power of Sa - tan break - ing,   Our peace e - ter - nal mak - ing.
zu den Sa - tan zwin - gen   Und al - les wie - der brin - gen.

IN PART II of Bach's *Christmas Oratorio,* the Evangelist sings, in recitative, the following lines (Luke 2:8-9):

And there were shepherds in the same country, abiding in the field, keeping watch over their flocks by night.

And lo, an angel of the Lord stood by them, and the glory of the Lord shone round about them, and they were sore afraid.

Then follows this glorious chorale, which the congregation was intended to sing in unison.

The words were composed by Johann Rist, a distinguished 17th-century German cleric, who published them in his *Himmlische Lieder* in 1641 with a tune by his music editor, Johann Schop, fiddler, trombonist, composer. Bach's version is based on Schop's tune, though somewhat remotely. The text was suggested by a passage in Isaiah: *For unto us a child is born . . . and the government shall be upon his shoulder: and his name shall be called . . . The Prince of Peace.*

I Heard the Bells on Christmas Day

Henry Wadsworth Longfellow (1807–1882)

Henry Bishop (ca. 1665–1737)

R.F.

1. I heard the bells on Christmas Day Their old fa - mil - iar car - ols play, And wild and sweet the words re - peat Of peace on earth, good will to men.

2. I thought how, as the day had come, The bel - fries of all Chris - ten - dom Had rolled a - long th'un - brok - en song Of peace on earth, good will to men.

3. And in de - spair I bowed my head; "There is no peace on earth," I said, "For hate is strong and mocks the song Of peace on earth, good will to men." will to men!

4. Then pealed the bells more loud and deep:
   "God is not dead, nor doth He sleep;
   The wrong shall fail, the right prevail,
   With peace on earth, good will to men."

5. Till, ringing, singing on its way,
   The world revolv'd from night to day,
   A voice, a chime, a chant sublime,
   Of peace on earth, good will to men!

LIKE ALMOST all of the Longfellow verses that have been found useful by hymn-makers, these were never intended to be a hymn at all. Yet they appear in many books of hymns and carols, set to various tunes. When Longfellow wrote the poem, in 1863, under the title of "Christmas Bells," his son had been seriously wounded as a lieutenant in the Army of the Potomac. The third stanza reflects his gloom—and also makes the carol peculiarly poignant during this, the sixth decade of the 20th century.

The tune, known as ILLSLEY in the hymnals, was already a century and a half old when Longfellow wrote his poem.

127

O LITTLE TOWN OF BETHLEHEM

Phillips Brooks (1835–1893)

Lewis H. Redner (1831–1908)

R.F.

1. O lit - tle town of Beth - le - hem, How still we _ see thee lie! A -
2. For Christ is born of Ma - ry, And gath - ered _ all a - bove, While

bove thy deep and dream - less sleep The si - lent _ stars go by; Yet
mor - tals sleep, the an - gels keep Their watch of _ won - d'ring love. O

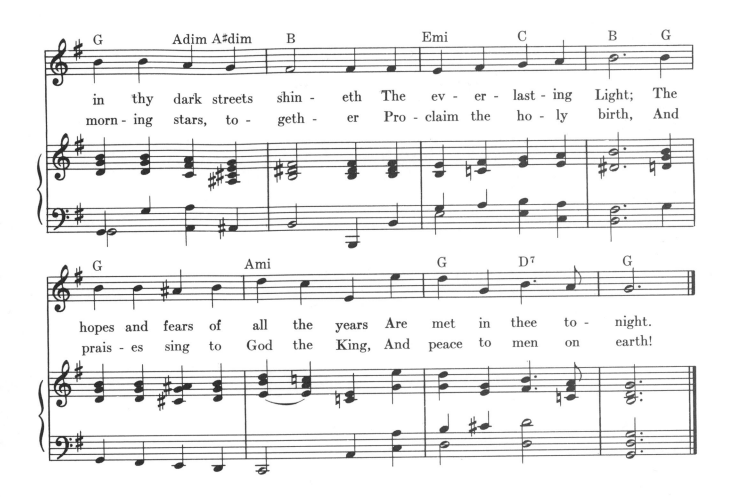

in thy dark streets shin - eth The ev - er - last - ing Light; The
morn - ing stars, to - geth - er Pro - claim the ho - ly birth, And

hopes and fears of all the years Are met in thee to - night.
prais - es sing to God the King, And peace to men on earth!

3. How silently, how silently,
   The wondrous gift is giv'n!
   So God imparts to human hearts
   The blessings of His heav'n.
   No ear may hear His coming,
   But in this world of sin,
   Where meek souls will receive Him still,
   The Dear Christ enters in.

4. O holy Child of Bethlehem,
   Descend to us, we pray;
   Cast out our sin and enter in;
   Be born in us today!
   We hear the Christmas angels
   The great glad tidings tell;
   O come to us, abide with us
   Our Lord Emmanuel!

THE AUTHOR of this carol was probably the most eloquent and highly respected of all the divines from Boston in the 19th century. Shortly before his death, he became Bishop of Massachusetts. At the age of thirty, he took a trip to the Holy Land, riding on horseback from Jerusalem to Bethlehem shortly before Christmas. It was this trip which is said to have inspired the verses. At any rate, he penned them three years later for the Christmas services in the Sunday School at Holy Trinity, Philadelphia, where he was rector. The church organist, who also conducted a class in the Sunday School, took the verses home on Saturday and had this famous setting for them ready for the next morning's classes.

FROM THE EASTERN MOUNTAINS

Godfrey Thring (1823–1903)

Arthur Henry Mann (1850–1929)

R.F.

1. From the east-ern moun-tains, Press-ing on they come, ___ Wise men in their wis - dom ___ To His _ hum - ble home; Stirred by deep de - vo - tion, Hast-ing from a - far, Ev - er jour-ney-ing on - ward,

2. There their Lord and Sav - iour Meek and low-ly lay, ___ Won-drous Light that lead them ___ On - ward_ on their way, Ev - er now to light - en Na - tions from a - far, As they jour - ney home - ward

REFRAIN:

Guid-ed by a star.
By that guid-ing star.

Light of Light that shin-eth Ere the world be-gan, ___ Draw Thou near, and light-en Ev-'ry heart of man.

3. Thou Who in a manger
Once hast lowly lain,
Who dost now in glory
O'er all kingdoms reign,
Gather in the people
Who in lands afar
Ne'er have seen the brightness
Of Thy guiding star.
Refrain:

4. Gather in the outcasts,
All who've gone astray,
Throw Thy radiance o'er them,
Guide them on their way,
Those who never knew Thee,
Those who've wandered far,
Lead them by the brightness
Of Thy guiding star.
Refrain:

5. Onward through the darkness
Of the lonely night,
Shining still before them
With Thy kindly light,
Guide them, Jew and Gentile,
Homeward from afar,
Young and old together,
By Thy guiding star.
Refrain:

6. Until every nation,
Whether bond or free,
'Neath Thy starlit banner,
Jesus, follows Thee
O'er the distant mountains
To that heav'nly home,
Where no sin nor sorrow
Ever more shall come.
Refrain:

IN NO CAROL from the folk-tune literature did the three magi ever make their famous pilgrimage with so firm a tread as in this confident mid-Victorian hymn. It was produced by two excellent scholars: Canon Thring was a highly regarded hymnologist and Arthur Mann a distinguished authority on Handel and a fine organist and choirmaster. The music makes an excellent processional for a spacious church; the sentiments and con-descending tone could perhaps only be achieved in a great and growing colonial empire.

The avowed inspiration is Matthew 2:2, ". . . we have seen his star in the east, and are come to worship him." The shadow of Herod's frightful political acts, which occupy much of the rest of the chapter, do not darken this Christmas poem.

How Brightly Shines the Morning Star

Wie schön leuchtet der Morgenstern

Philipp Nicolai (1556–1608)

Philipp Nicolai
harmonized by J. S. Bach
H.W.S.

1. How bright-ly shines the morn-ing star, With mer-cy beam-ing from a - far; The
Wie schön leuch-tet der Mor-gen-stern Voll Gnad und Wahr-heit von dem Herrn, Die

host of heav'n re - joi - ces; O Right-eous Branch, O Jes - se's Rod! Thou
süs - se Wur - zel Jes - se! Du Sohn Da - vid aus Ja - kobs Stamm, Mein

Son of man and Son of God! We, too, will lift our voi - ces:
Kö - nig und mein Bräu - ti - gam, Hast mir mein Herz be - ses - sen.

A - men, A - men! Ho - ly, ho - ly, yet most low - ly,
Lieb - lich, freund - lich, Schön und herr - lich, gross und ehr - lich,

Draw Thou near us; Great Em - man - uel, come and hear us.
Reich von Ga - ben, Hoch und sehr präch - tig er - ha - ben.

2. Rejoice, ye heav'ns; thou earth, reply;
With praise, ye sinners, fill the sky,
For this His incarnation.
Incarnate God, put forth Thy power,
Ride on, ride on, great Conqueror,
Till all know Thy salvation.
Amen, Amen! Hallelujah! Hallelujah!
Praise be given
Evermore, by earth and heaven.

THE STORY goes that during the great pestilence of 1597, the sturdy pastor Nicolai was one morning especially distressed by all the death he found among his parishioners. But rising from his distress, he suddenly felt greatly inspired by his love for the Saviour. In a kind of religious ecstasy, he forgot everything around him and wrote these verses (and probably the tune too) in three hours. There were seven stanzas in the original German, and their first letters formed an acrostic on the name of Count Waldeck, Nicolai's aristocratic friend and pupil.

Nicolai called it "a spiritual bridal song of the believing soul concerning Jesus Christ, her heavenly bridegroom, founded on the 45th Psalm of the prophet David." Accordingly, it has often been used as a wedding hymn. It has also been widely used at funerals; and in some towns of Germany the city chimes were set to the tune, known as "the queen of chorales." Bach, however, whose harmonization is always used nowadays, introduced it in his *Cantata No. 1 for the Feast of the Annunciation,* and some hymnals place it, accordingly, in the Christmas section. That is enough excuse, if any is needed, for including so beautiful a piece in our book.

O COME, O COME, EMMANUEL

Veni, Emmanuel

Latin, 12th century
translated by John M. Neale

Plain Song, 12th century
H.W.S.

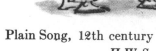

1. O come, O come, Em- man- u- el, And ran- som cap- tive Is- ra- el,
1. Ve- ni, ve- ni, Em- ma- nu- el, Cap- ti- vum sol- ve Is- ra- el,

That mourns in lone- ly ex- ile here Un- til the Son of God__ ap- pear.
Qui ge- mit in ex- i- li- o, Pri- va- tus De- i fi- li- o.

REFRAIN:

Re- joice! Re- joice! Em- man- u- el Shall come to thee, O Is- ra- el.
Gau- de, gau- de, Em- ma- nu- el Nas- ce- tur pro te, Is- ra- el.

2. O come, O come, Thou Rod of Jesse, free
Thine own from Satan's tyranny;
From depths of hell Thy people save,
And give them victory o'er the grave.
Refrain:

3. O come, Thou Dayspring, come and cheer
Our spirits by Thine advent here;
Disperse the gloomy clouds of night,
And death's dark shadows put to flight.
Refrain:

4. O come, Thou Key of David, come,
And open wide our heav'nly home;
Make safe the way that leads on high,
And close the path to misery.
Refrain:

5. O come, O come, Thou Lord of might,
Who once, from Sinai's flaming height
Didst give the trembling tribes Thy law,
In cloud, and majesty, and awe.
Refrain:

2. *Veni, O Iesse virgula,*
Ex hostis tuos ungula,
De specu tuos Tartari
Educ, et antro barathri.
Refrain:

3. *Veni, veni, O Oriens,*
Solare nos adveniens:
Noctis depelle nebulas,
Dirasque noctis tenebras.
Refrain:

4. *Veni, clavis Davidica,*
Regna reclude caelica,
Fac iter tutum superum,
Et claude vias inferum.
Refrain:

5. *Veni, veni, Adonai,*
Qui populo in Sinai
Legem dedisti vertice,
In maiestate gloriae.
Refrain:

Therefore the Lord himself shall give you a sign: Behold, a virgin shall conceive, and bear a son, and shall call his name Immanuel. Isaiah 7:14

SO SAID the prophet Isaiah, mentioning the name Immanuel for the first time in the Old Testament. Matthew quotes him in the New Testament (1:23), adding the meaning of "Immanuel": *which being interpreted is, God with us.*

On December 17 in medieval monasteries, the abbot would intone the original first stanza at vespers, both before and after the Magnificat. On successive evenings, each of the principal officers of the monastery would take his turn with another of the stanzas, the whole series being known as the "Seven O's." Each O hailed the coming Saviour under a different epithet: *O Sapientia, O Adonai,* etc. After the service, the officer was expected to stand some sort of treat, usually edible, for all the monks. The prayer, despite the solemnity to modern ears that lies in the modal plain song, was rightly joyful.

The particular plain song always associated nowadays with these verses is, historically, a congeries of several *Kyrie*'s put together in the 19th century by Thomas Helmore to use with John M. Neale's translation. One can best get the illusion of medieval monastic celebration by chanting the hymn unaccompanied in unison, and without too strict a regard for the four-square metrics of the modern musical transcription.

While by My Sheep I Watched at Night
Als ich bei meinen Schafen wacht

Old German
English version by Theodore Baker

Old German
H.W.S.

While by my sheep I watched at night, Glad ti - dings brought an
Als ich bei mei - nen Scha - fen wacht, Ein En - gel mir die

2. There shall be born, so he did say,
   In Bethlehem a Child today.

3. There shall He lie, in manger mean,
   Who shall redeem the world from sin.

4. Lord, evermore to me be nigh,
   Then shall my heart be filled with joy!

2. *Er sagt es soll geboren sein*
   Zu Bethlehem ein Kindlein.

3. *Er sagt das Kind läg da im Stall*
   Und sollt die Welt erlösen all.

4. *Den Schatz muss ich bewahren wohl,*
   So bleibt mein Herz der Freude voll.

WITH THE EXCEPTION of the final echo, which is not included at all, the German words and the tune are given as they appear in a famous 17th-century collection. They are certainly still older, having been originally composed, in all probability, for a medieval Christmas pageant. Dr. Baker's translation is used because it is eminently singable and widely familiar. It omits, however, five charmingly naïve stanzas in which the shepherd relates how the Christ Child transfixed his eye, how he kissed the tiny feet (which tasted like sugar), how the Child wished to go with him, and how he finally laid Him joyfully on his heart.

WATCHMAN, TELL US OF THE NIGHT

Sir John Bowring (1792–1872)

? Jakob Hintze (1622–1702)
harmonized by J. S. Bach
H.W.S.

Traveller
1. Watch - man, tell us of the night, What its signs of prom - ise are.
2. Watch - man, tell us of the night, High - er yet that star as - cends.
3. Watch - man, tell us of the night, For the morn - ing seems to dawn.

Watchman
Trav - 'ler, o'er yon moun - tain's height, See that glo - ry - beam - ing star.
Trav - 'ler, bless - ed - ness and light, Peace and truth its course por - tends.
Trav - 'ler, dark - ness takes its flight, Doubt and ter - ror are with - drawn.

Traveller
Watch - man, does its beau - teous ray Aught of joy or hope fore - tell?
Watch - man, will its beams a - lone Gild the spot that gave them birth?
Watch - man, let thy wand' - rings cease; Hie thee to thy qui - et home:

IN LATER LIFE, Sir John Bowring was to become a distinguished member of Parliament, an orientalist, and Governor of Hongkong. But when he penned these lines, he was still the young editor of the *Westminster Review,* passionately interested in social and political reform. The verses are sung often to a slightly jigging waltz tune by Lowell Mason.

We prefer the more solemn setting, especially when decked out in the harmonies of the Bach chorale. Actually, the first set of words for the tune were not only solemn but rather lugubrious, beginning *Alle Menschen müssen sterben* (All men must die). It appeared, anonymously, in the 1678 edition of the *Praxis pietatis melica,* and it was not until five editions later that the initials of Jakob Hintze, the learned editor of this German collection, were added to the tune. Hence the question mark before his name.

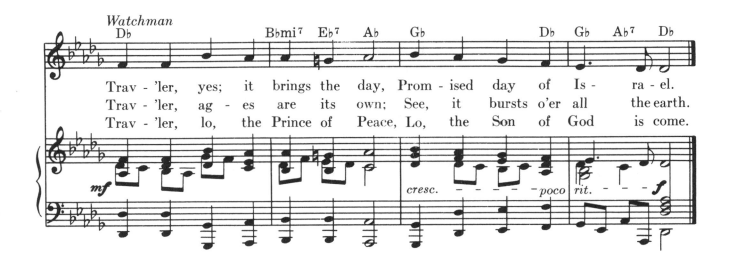

Watchman

| | Db | | | | | | Bbmi7 | Eb7 | Ab | Gb | | | | Db | Gb | Ab7 | Db |

Trav - 'ler, yes; it brings the day, Prom - ised day of Is - ra - el.
Trav - 'ler, ag - es are its own; See, it bursts o'er all the earth.
Trav - 'ler, lo, the Prince of Peace, Lo, the Son of God is come.

mf

cresc. — — — — -poco rit. — — -f

SHOUT THE GLAD TIDINGS

William A. Muhlenberg (1796–1877)

Charles Avison (*ca.* 1710–1770)
R.F.

Shout the glad ti - dings, ex - ult - ing - ly sing; _____ Je - ru - sa - lem tri - umphs, Mes - si - ah is King!

1. Zi - on, the mar - vel - ous
2. Tell how He com - eth; from

3. Mortals, your homage be gratefully bringing,
And sweet let the gladsome hosanna arise:
Ye angels, the full alleluia be singing;
One chorus resound through the earth and the skies.

After last stanza only

Shout the glad ti-dings, ex-ult-ing-ly sing; _____ Je - ru - sa - lem

tri-umphs, Mes - si - ah is King, Mes - si - ah is King, Mes - si - ah is King!

CHARLES AVISON is one of those thousands of competent composers one finds in the history of music who are nothing but entries in an encyclopedia a hundred years after their deaths. Browning, in a long imaginary conversation with Avison (a section of his *Parleyings with Certain People of Importance in Their Day*) attributed Avison's lack of fashion to the effect of Wagner's revolutionary harmonizing. Yet, oddly enough, now in mid-20th century, there is a revival of interest in the sonatas and concertos of the organist of Newcastle-upon-Tyne. They are being dusted off in England, replayed, and even republished.

The present tune, which comes from one of Avison's concertos,

alone remained popular for at least fifty years after his death, when it was sung, on both sides of the Atlantic, to a paraphrase of the *Song of Miriam* by Tom Moore. It began:

Sound the loud timbrel o'er Egypt's dark sea:
Jehova has triumphed, his people go free.

Shout the Glad Tidings was written by the rector of St. George's in Flushing, Long Island, especially to be sung at the Christmas services of 1826 in Trinity Church, New York. Bishop Hobart was enthusiastic about the verses, and they were immediately incorporated into the new Episcopalian hymnal of that year. Since then they have been added to many other hymnals.

Calm on the Listening Ear
of Night

Edmund H. Sears (1810–1876)

John Bacchus Dykes (1823–1876)

R.F.

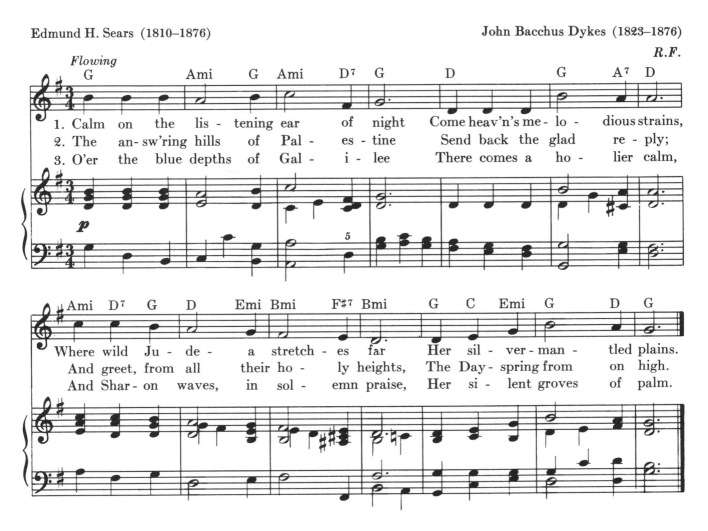

1. Calm on the lis - tening ear of night Come heav'n's me - lo - dious strains,
2. The an - sw'ring hills of Pal - es - tine Send back the glad re - ply;
3. O'er the blue depths of Gal - i - lee There comes a ho - lier calm,

Where wild Ju - de - a stretch - es far Her sil - ver - man - tled plains.
And greet, from all their ho - ly heights, The Day - spring from on high.
And Shar - on waves, in sol - emn praise, Her si - lent groves of palm.

4. "Glory to God!" the sounding skies
   Loud with their anthems ring,
   "Peace to the earth, goodwill to men,
   From heav'ns eternal King!"

5. Light on thy hills, Jerusalem!
   The Saviour now is born:
   More bright on Bethlehem's joyous plains
   Breaks the first Christmas morn.

THE WIDELY beloved lines are fifteen years older than the author's most famous Christmas song, *It Came Upon a Midnight Clear* (see p. 122). Sears composed them shortly after he entered the Harvard Divinity School, at the age of twenty-five.

The prolific British divine, John Bacchus Dykes, composed a score of tunes that still appear in practically every Protestant hymnal. The present one, known as ST. AGNES, has had a somewhat wayward history. It was originally composed for the hymn *Jesus, the Very Thought of Thee*. That translation from an anonymous Latin source, however, is more often sung to any one of three other tunes; while the calm, quiet warmth of ST. AGNES has prompted its use not only for our Christmas hymn but also for *Come, Holy Spirit, Heavenly Dove* and the anonymous *Shepherd of Souls*.

ANGELS, FROM THE REALMS OF GLORY

James Montgomery (1771–1854)

Henry Thomas Smart (1813–1879)

R.F.

1. An - gels, from the realms of glo - ry, Wing your flight o'er all the earth;
2. Shep - herds, in the fields a - bid - ing, Watch-ing o'er your flocks by night,

Ye who sang cre - a - tion's sto - ry, Now pro - claim Mes - si - ah's birth:
God with man is now re - sid - ing, Yon - der shines the ___ in - fant Light:

Come and wor - ship, Come and wor - ship, Wor - ship Christ, the new - born King!

3. Sages, leave your contemplations,
   Brighter visions beam afar;
   Seek the great Desire of nations;
   Ye have seen His natal star:
   Come and worship, Come and worship,
   Worship Christ, the newborn King!

4. Saints, before the altar bending,
   Watching long in hope and fear,
   Suddenly the Lord, descending,
   In His temple shall appear:
   Come and worship, Come and worship,
   Worship Christ, the newborn King!

THE AUTHOR of these verses was, from childhood, one of those idealistic, liberal, militant rebels who helped form the best of the sturdy decency in early Victorian British character. Scots-born orphan of an illiterate Irish peasant, he was expelled from school for spending too much time writing poetry. Next he became apprenticed to a baker; but he found his life's work when one Gales, auctioneer, bookseller, and publisher, employed him to work on the *Sheffield Register*. When Gales's politics forced him into exile, Montgomery, aged twenty-three, took over the paper, altered its name to *The Iris*—and presently found himself in political trouble too. He was harshly criticized for opposing the slave trade, and he found himself in prison for celebrating,

in verse, the fall of the Bastille. Yet before he died, he had been invited to lecture on poetry at the conservative Royal Institute, and he is remembered today as the author of a baker's dozen of hymns that appear in Protestant hymnals.

The tune most frequently used today with Montgomery's verses was composed thirteen years after his death by a highly respected church organist and organ-designer who composed one successful opera and a great deal of other music. The present tune is his most enduring contribution: its vigorous, cheerful self-confidence has inspired its adoption as the tune for many a set of hymn verses besides these. You will find it listed in the hymnals under the name of REGENT SQUARE.

Joy to the World!

Isaac Watts (1674–1748)

Unknown
R.F.

Vigorously

1. Joy to the world! the Lord is come; Let earth re-ceive her King; Let
2. Joy to the world! the Sav-iour reigns; Let men their songs em-ploy; While
3. He rules the world with truth and grace, And makes the na-tions prove The

THIS FAMOUS tune appeared first in an English hymnal, and it is customarily ascribed to Handel. But as Handel did not write it, some early tune-detective racked his brain and came up with the assertion that it is made up of two numbers from the *Messiah*—the chorus *Lift Up Your Hearts* and a portion of the tenor recitative *Comfort Ye, My People*. Many tired commentators have repeated this conjecture. Yet, the second attribution is so distant as to be virtually unrecognizable; and the first is confined to the four opening notes. Many other tunes by many composers start with four descending notes; and one might as well say that the unknown composer had helped himself to the opening of the popular love song *Caro mio ben*, probably by the 18th-century Giuseppi Giordani. The simple truth seems to be that the tune was composed by that highly gifted and versatile creative talent *Anon*. Whoever he was, he wrote a tune admirably suited to the joyous words of Watts, and he arranged a portion of it in the "fuguing" manner so popular in the 18th century and still attractive today.

The inspiration of Watts may be much more reliably reported. He published the verses in 1719 as part of the *Psalms of David, Imitated in the Language of the New Testament.* This is the relevant part of the 98th Psalm:

> *Make a joyful noise unto the Lord, all the earth: make a*
> *loud noise, and rejoice, and sing praise . . .*
> *. . . for he cometh to judge the earth . . .*

O COME, ALL YE FAITHFUL

Adeste, fideles

(?) John Francis Wade (1712–1786)

(?) John Reading (d. 1692)

R.F.

DURING the troublous times of the 1740's, many an English Catholic sympathizer with the cause of the Stuarts found himself in or near Douay in France. There, one John Francis Wade plied his trade as a music copyist, producing manuscripts that were praised for their beauty. At least six copies of the words of this hymn have been found in various places in England and Ireland, all in Wade's hand and set to music quite different from ours, in triple time. It is perfectly possible that Wade composed the hymn himself, for he signed it *(Ad usum chori Anglorum—Johannes Franciscus Wade scripsit);* yet the hymn's comparatively early and consistent popularity in France and Wade's trade as copyist suggest that it may belong to an anonymous Frenchman. As for the translation, Julian's *Dictionary of Hym-*

nology lists several dozen in English. The present and by much the most widely used one is the result of much tinkering, by many hands, with one that originally began, "Ye faithful, approach ye."

Many hymnals label the tune "Portuguese Hymn." That is because its earliest known use to these words occurred in the chapel of the Portuguese Embassy in London toward the close of the 18th century. The organist of the chapel was Vincent Novello, an English composer with many literary friends. He ascribed the tune to the eldest of three John Readings, all English composers. Novello's nominee had been organist at Winchester College a hundred years earlier, and although some of his compositions are still in print, this is not among them.

2. Sing, choirs of angels, sing in exultation,
   O sing, all ye citizens of heaven above!
   Glory to God, all glory in the highest;
   O come, let us adore Him,
   O come, let us adore Him,
   O come, let us adore Him, Christ, the Lord!

3. Yea, Lord, we greet Thee, born this happy morning,
   Jesus, to Thee be all glory giv'n;
   Word of the Father, now in flesh appearing;
   O come, let us adore Him,
   O come, let us adore Him,
   O come, let us adore Him, Christ, the Lord!

2. Cantet nunc Io chorus angelorum,
   Cantet nunc aula caelestium:
   Gloria, gloria in excelsis Deo:
   Venite adoremus, venite adoremus,
   Venite adoremus Dominum.

3. Ergo qui natus die hodierna,
   Iesu, tibi sit gloria:
   Patris aeterni verbum caro factum:
   Venite adoremus, venite adoremus,
   Venite adoremus Dominum.

FROM HEAVEN HIGH

Vom Himmel hoch

Martin Luther (1483–1546)

translated by Catherine Winkworth

attributed to Martin Luther

harmonized by J. S. Bach

H.W.S.

1. From heav-en high I come to you, To bring you ti-dings_ strange and true. Glad ti-dings of_ great joy _ I bring, Where-of I now will_ say_ and sing.

2. To you this night is born a Child Of Ma-ry, cho-sen_Moth-er mild; This lit-tle Child, of low-ly birth, Shall be the joy of _ all _ the earth.

3. Glo-ry to God in high-est heaven,Who un-to us His_ Son hath given! While an-gels sing with pi-ous mirth, A glad New Year to _ all _ the earth.

1. *Vom Himmel hoch, da komm ich her,*
Ich bring' euch gute neue Mär,
Der guten Mär bring' ich so viel,
Davon ich sing'n und sagen will.

2. *Euch ist ein Kindlein heut' gebor'n,*
Von einer Jungfrau auserkor'n,
Ein Kindelein so zart und fein,
Das soll eu'r Freud' und Wonne sein.

3. *Lob, Ehr' sei Gott im höchsten Thron,*
Der uns schenkt seinen ein'gen Sohn,
Des freuen sich der Engel Schar
Und singen uns solch neues Jahr.

THOUGH Martin Luther is customarily—and appropriately enough—credited with both the poem and the tune of this famous German chorale, its ultimate origin is probably older than he. The first stanza is really a paraphrase of a much older song beginning:

Ich komm aus fremden Landen her
Und bring euch viel der neuen Mähr.

When Luther first published his version, he did it to the tune that had been associated with this folk poem. Four years later, in 1539, Luther's poem was printed with the present superb melody—which Luther may or may not have composed. At any rate, the chorale was apparently prepared by him first for the use of his own family at a Christmas celebration and intended to be sung in unison.

In Bach's *Christmas Oratorio,* he makes use of this chorale in three different harmonizations, one more elaborate than the other. We use the first and simplest of these versions, faithfully following his harmonies but omitting the orchestral interlude after every line.

HOW SHALL I FITLY MEET THEE?

Wie soll ich Dich empfangen?

"Picander" (1700–1764)

Hans Leo Hassler (1564–1612)
harmonized by J. S. Bach

H.W.S.

How shall I fit - ly meet Thee, And give Thee wel - come due? The
Wie soll ich Dich emp - fang - en, Und wie be - geg - nen Dir? O

na - tions long to greet Thee, And I would greet Thee, too. O
al - ler Welt Ver - lang - en, O mei - ner See - le Zier! O

Fount of light, shine bright - ly Up - on my dark - ened heart, That
Je - su, Je - su! Set - ze Mir selbst die Fak - kel bei, Da -

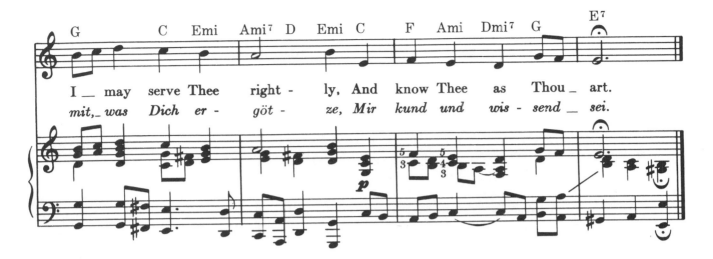

THIS IS the first of the chorales in Bach's *Christmas Oratorio* and is deeply expressive of the awe and wonder with which a simple shepherd—or possibly Joseph—might have contemplated the birth of the Saviour. Immediately after the congregation sings it in unison, the Evangelist (or Narrator) sings a recitative based on Luke 2:7—

> And she brought forth her first-born Son, and she wrapped Him in swaddling clothes, and laid Him in a manger.

The oratorio, a series of six cantatas for different days during Christmastime, was composed in 1734 to words compiled and written by Christian Friedrich Henrici (a Leipzig postal official who used the pen name of "Picander") and Bach himself. The tune, composed over a century earlier by the Nürnberger Hassler, was one that haunted Bach. Five years earlier, in the great *St. Thomas Passion,* he had harmonized it five different ways. The present harmonization is again quite different. Its strange closing, on a dominant chord, has, in the words of Sir George Macfarren, who edited the *Christmas Oratorio,* "a great power of suggestion as to what may be the result of man's meeting with the Saviour."

While Shepherds Watched Their Flocks By Night

Nahum Tate (1652-1715)

George Frideric Handel (1685-1759)

R.F.

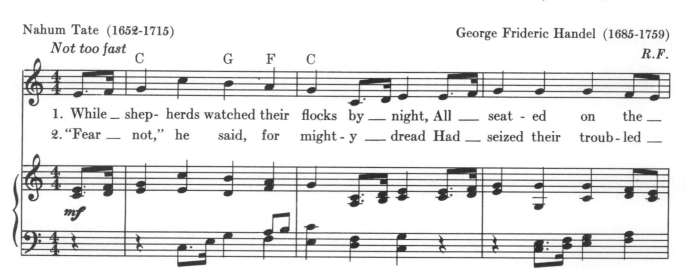

1. While __ shep- herds watched their flocks by __ night, All __ seat- ed   on   the __
2. "Fear __ not," he   said, for   might- y __ dread Had __ seized their   troub- led __

ground, ___ The __ an - gel of the Lord came __ down, And __
mind, ___ "Glad __ ti - dings of great joy I __ bring To __

glo - ry shone a - round, _____ And glo - ry shone a - round.
you and all man - kind. _____ To you and all man - kind.

3. "To you, in David's town, this day,
Is born of David's line,
The Saviour, who is Christ, the Lord,
And this shall be the sign,
And this shall be the sign;

4. "The heavenly Babe you there shall find
To human view displayed,
And meanly wrapped in swathing bands,
And in a manger laid,
And in a manger laid."

5. Thus spake the seraph and forthwith
Appeared a shining throng
Of angels, praising God, who thus
Addressed their joyful song,
Addressed their joyful song:

6. "All glory be to God on high,
And to the earth be peace;
Goodwill henceforth from heav'n to men
Begin, and never cease,
Begin, and never cease!"

WHEN these verses first appeared in 1708 in England, they constituted the only Christmas hymn officially sanctioned by the Church of England for use in divine service. They are the work of Nahum Tate, the poet laureate, and appeared as part of a supplement to the so-called *New Version of the Psalms* by "Dr. Brady and Mr. Tate." Entitled "Song of the Angels," the carol was inspired by eight verses from the second chapter of Luke, beginning: "And there were in the same country shepherds abiding in the field, keeping watch over their flock by night."
The carol is sometimes sung to the tune by Richard Willis that we most often use for *It Came Upon a Midnight Clear* (see p. 122). The present setting, the most common one for it in America, is a close adaptation of a soprano aria from *Siroë, King of Persia,* a thoroughly secular opera produced by Handel in London in 1728. In this aria, a princess, dressed as a man, finds herself obliged to make love to a woman. The princess wishes she might have been born a shepherdess to avoid such grievous embarrassment. . . . Which only goes to show that a good tune may serve many purposes.

BESIDE THY CRADLE HERE I STAND

Ich steh an Deiner Krippe hier

Paul Gerhardt (1607–1676)

J. S. Bach (1685–1750)

H.W.S.

Be - side Thy cra - dle here I stand, O __ Thou that ev - er __ liv - est,
Ich steh an Dei - ner Krip - pe hier, O __ Je - sus - lein, mein Le - ben.

And bring Thee with a will - ing hand The __ ver - y gifts Thou __ giv - est.
Ich ste - he, bring und schen - ke Dir Was __ Du mir hast ge - ge - ben.

Ac - cept me: 'tis my mind __ and heart, My soul, my strength, my
Nimm hin, es ist mein Geist __ und Sinn, Herz, Seel' und Mut, nimm

ev - ery part That Thou from me re - quir - est.
al - les hin, Und lass Dir's wohl ge - fal - len.

IN THE FINAL SECTION of the *Christmas Oratorio,* the Evangelist narrates the story of the three magi. "Falling down, they worshipped Him," he sings, "and having opened their treasures, they offered Him gold, frankincense, and myrrh." Then the congregation sings our chorale, and the story is taken up again.

Bach and Picander, putting Gerhardt's poem at this place, suggest that it represents the emotions of awe and tenderness which must have struck the three wise men on that first Epiphany. Bach was greatly taken with the poem, and two years later he set it to music once more, as an aria for soprano.

HARK! THE HERALD ANGELS SING

Charles Wesley (1707–1788)

Felix Mendelssohn-Bartholdy (1809–1847)

R.F.

With festal pomp

1. Hark! the her - ald an - gels sing, ___ "Glo - ry to the new - born King;
2. Christ, by high - est heaven a - dored; ___ Christ, the ev - er - last - ing Lord;

Peace on earth, and mer - cy mild, ___ God and sin - ners rec - on - ciled!"
Come, De - sire of Na - tions, come, ___ Fix in us thy hum - ble home.

Joy - ful, all ye na - tions, rise, ___ Join the tri - umph of the skies; ___
Veiled in flesh the God - head see; ___ Hail th'In - car - nate De - i - ty, ___

With th'an - gel - ic hosts pro - claim, "Christ is ___ born in Beth - le - hem!"
Pleased as man with man to dwell; Je - sus, ___ our Em - man - u - el.

REFRAIN:

Hark! the her - ald an - gels sing, "Glo - ry ___ to the new-born King."

3. Hail, the heav'n-born Prince of Peace!
   Hail, the Sun of Righteousness!
   Light and life to all He brings,
   Ris'n with healing in His wings;
   Mild He lays His glory by,
   Born that man no more may die,
   Born to raise the sons of earth,
   Born to give them second birth;

   Refrain:

OF THE MORE than four thousand hymns published by the co-founder of Methodism during his lifetime, and the more than two thousand left in manuscript, this is probably the most famous of all. (Other widely popular hymns written by Charles Wesley include *Jesus, Lover of My Soul; Love Divine, All Loves Excelling; Christ the Lord Is Risen Today;* and *Soldiers of Christ, Arise.*) Oddly enough, *Hark! the Herald Angels* is also the one that has been most extensively altered from the author's original version, which began:

> Hark, how all the welkin rings
> "Glory to the King of Kings."

Wesley was irritated.

Mendelssohn, though a remarkably even-tempered gentleman,

might also have been irritated had he lived to learn to what use his music had been put. It originally formed the second movement of a choral work entitled, *For a Tercentenary of the Invention of the Art of Printing.* The movement praised the work of "Gutenberg, the German man," and Mendelssohn thought that if only better words were found, the tune might become quite popular. However, he added, "It will *never* do to sacred words." How right he was in the first part of his prediction, how wrong in his qualification!

In the original Mendelssohn, the melody was sung by male voices in unison excepting a few bars in thirds. Words and tune were first united in 1855, by William H. Cummings, when the composer had been dead for eight years, the author for sixty-seven.

Especially for Children

O Come, Little Children

Ihr Kinderlein, kommet

Christoph von Schmid (1768–1854)

J. A. P. Schulz (1747–1800)

R.F.

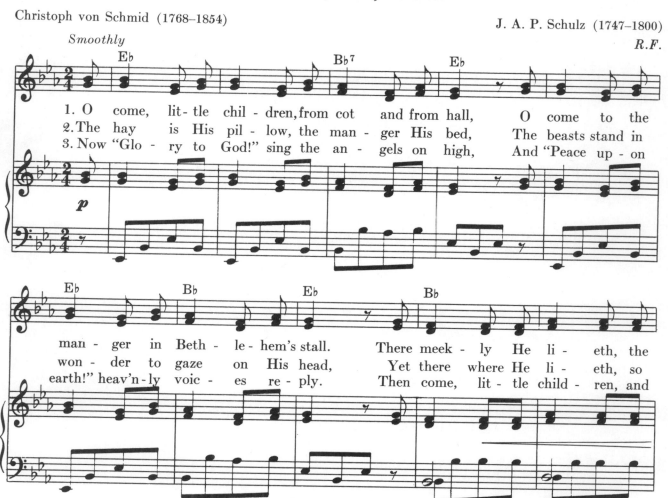

1. O come, lit- tle chil- dren, from cot and from hall, O come to the man- ger in Beth- le- hem's stall. There meek- ly He li - eth, the
2. The hay is His pil - low, the man - ger His bed, The beasts stand in won- der to gaze on His head, Yet there where He li - eth, so
3. Now "Glo - ry to God!" sing the an - gels on high, And "Peace up - on earth!" heav'n- ly voic - es re - ply. Then come, lit - tle child - ren, and

heav - en - ly Child,   So poor and so hum - ble, so sweet and so mild.
weak and so poor,   Come shep-herds and wise men to kneel at His door.
join in the lay   That glad - dened the world on that first Christ-mas Day.

1. *Ihr Kinderlein, kommet, o kommet doch all!*
   Zur Krippe her kommet in Bethlehem's Stall,
   Und seht was in dieser hochheiligen Nacht
   Der Vater im Himmel für Freude uns macht.

2. *Da liegt es, ach Kinder, auf Heu und auf Stroh,*
   Maria und Josef betrachten es froh;
   Die redlichen Hirten knien betend davor,
   Hoch oben schwebt jubelnd der Engelein Chor.

3. *O beugt, wie die Hirten, anbetend die Knie,*
   Erhebet die Händlein und danket wie sie!
   Stimmt freudig, ihr Kinder, wer sollt' sich nicht freu'n?
   Stimmt freudig zum Jubel der Engel mit ein.

JOHANN ABRAHAM PETER SCHULZ was a thorough, all-round German musician who studied with a pupil of J. S. Bach's, edited a music encyclopedia, wrote a book on harmony, composed operas for the Danish court (including a *Barber of Seville* that preceded Rossini's but followed Paisiello's), and was highly esteemed by his contemporaries.

His chief contribution to music, however, lay in his insistence on a high poetic quality in the songs that he set. At one time, these songs were widely sung in Germany and Denmark, most of them to verses by his contemporaries. *O Come, Little Children* represents the simple, romantic best achieved by these songs. Its author specialized in books on religion and moral instruction for the young.

The alto part is entirely optional.

THE CHRISTMAS TREE

O Tannenbaum

probably Westphalian
paraphrase by H.W.S.

possibly an old Catholic hymn
R.F.

1. We stand be-fore the Christ-mas tree, A sym-bol for the faith-ful:
1. O Tan - nen-baum, O Tan - nen-baum, Wie treu sind dei - ne Blät- ter!

Its fol- iage green will al-ways grow Through sum-mer sun and win- ter snow:
Du grünst nicht nur zur Som-mers-zeit, Nein, auch im Win - ter, wenn es schneit.

| F | | Cmi⁷ | D⁷ | | Gmi D⁷ Gmi | C⁷ | F |

We stand be-fore the Christ-mas tree, A sym-bol for the faith-ful.
O Tan - nen-baum, O Tan - nen-baum, Wie treu sind dei - ne Blät - ter!

2. And, oh, the Christmas tree can be
A source of simple pleasure:
To every girl and every boy
It speaks of holidays and joy:
Ah yes, the Christmas tree can be
A source of simple pleasure.

2. *O Tannenbaum, O Tannenbaum,*
Du kannst mir sehr gefallen.
Wie oft hat nicht zur Weihnachtszeit
Ein Baum von dir mich hoch erfreut!
O Tannenbaum, O Tannenbaum,
Du kannst mir sehr gefallen.

THE "PROBABLY" and the "possibly" at the head of the page indicate that the origin of this carol is as obscure as the origin of the festal symbolism of the fir tree. In Germany it remains one of the best loved of all the carols. In English-speaking countries it has always been less popular, probably because it is so difficult to make a translation that does not sound downright simple-minded. The German words are naïve in the extreme, and none of the dozen translations I have examined capture their childlike simplicity. That is why I have tried a paraphrase rather than a translation. I am not much pleased with the result and advise everyone to sing the German words. Alternately, one might use *Maryland, My Maryland.*

AWAY IN A MANGER

Anonymous

possibly by James R. Murray (1841?–1904)
H.W.S.

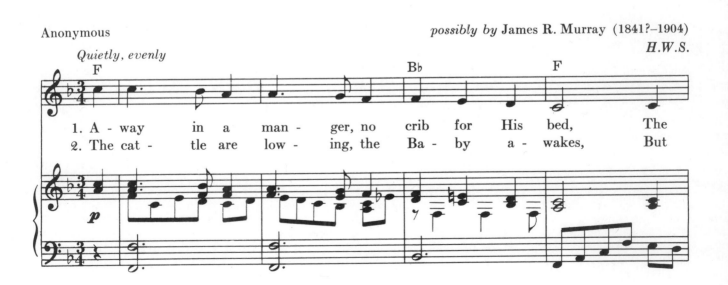

1. A - way in a man - ger, no crib for His bed, The
2. The cat - tle are low - ing, the Ba - by a - wakes, But

lit - tle Lord Je - sus laid down His sweet head. The
lit - tle Lord Je - sus, no cry - ing He makes. I

stars in the sky _____ looked down where He lay, The
love Thee, Lord Je - sus, look down from the sky, And

lit - tle Lord Je - sus, a - sleep on the hay.
stay by my cra - dle till morn - ing is nigh.

IN 1887 James R. Murray published a volume entitled *Dainty Songs for Little Lads and Lasses.* This tune and poem appeared in it under the heading *Luther's Cradle Hymn (Composed by Martin Luther for his children and still sung by German mothers to their little ones).* Despite the fact that Murray signed it with his initials, subsequent editors took the heading at face value and most collections of carols still ascribe words and music to Luther; this despite the fact that neither words nor tune bears the slightest resemblance to Luther's style and that the carol is virtually unknown in Germany—or anywhere else

outside the U.S.A.

In a highly diverting and scholarly piece of detective work, published in *Notes* by the Library of Congress a few years ago, Richard S. Hill exposed the pious fraud. He traced the first appearance of the poem to a *Little Children's Book,* published in 1885 by the Evangelical Lutheran Church in North America, where it appeared unsigned. He also uncovered some forty different musical settings for the poem. Our tune is the one most commonly used today, though AFTON WATERS *(Flow Gently, Sweet Afton)* is a close runner-up.

NOW IT IS CHRISTMASTIME

Nu är det Jul igen

Traditional Swedish
translated by H.W.S.

Traditional Swedish
H.W.S.

Gaily with marked rhythm

Now it is Christ-mas-time, va - ca - tion will start a - gain, and
Nu är det Jul i - gen, och nu är det Jul i - gen, och

ho - li - days will last till East - er;
Ju - len va - ra ska' till Pås - ka.

Then, when it's East - er - time, va - ca - tion will start a - gain, and
Så är det Påsk i - gen, och så är det Påsk i - gen, och

ho - li - days go on till Christ - mas.
Påsk - en va - ra ska' till Ju - la.

Now it is Christ - mas - time, va - ca - tion will start a - gain, and
Nu är det Jul i - gen, och nu är det Jul i - gen, och

ho - li - days will last till East - er;
Ju - len va - ra ska' till Pås - ka.

But it is not so; oh dear, it is not so, For
Det var in - te sant, och det var in - te sant, För

in | be - tween | there's | Lent | with | fast - | ing.
där | *e - mel -* | *lan* | *kom -* | *mer* | *Fas -* | *tan.*

ONE OF the most popular of Swedish folk dances is the hambo, danced to this tune. At Christmastime it is danced around the tree, mostly by children singing these repetitious, gaily nonsensical verses.

JINGLE BELLS

John Pierpont (1785–1866)

John Pierpont
R.F.

Dash - ing through the snow, In a one - horse o - pen sleigh,

O'er the fields we go, Laugh - ing all the way;

STRICTLY SPEAKING, this little ditty that everyone has known since he was so high does not belong in the book: there is no specific reference to Christmas in it. But children love to sing it, even if nowadays they are more likely to be riding in a closed car than in an open sleigh. R.F.'s arrangement is made for children: any tot should be able to pick out at least the right-hand part.

Prayer to the Child Jesus

Gebet an den heiligen Christ

German
translated by R.F.

German
R.F.

1. O ho - ly In - fant, small and dear, Your birth - day
1. *Du lie - ber, heil' - ger, from - mer Christ, Weil heu - te*

once a-gain __ is __ here, And joy-ful songs __ ring __
Dein Ge-burts-tag __ ist, Drum ist auf Er-den __

near and far Where-ev-er lit-tle __ child-ren are.
weit und breit Bei al-len Kin-dern __ fro-he Zeit.

2. O bless me, I am still a child;
   O cleanse my heart and make it mild,
   And in Your pure and heavenly spring,
   O lave my soul and make it sing.

2. O segne mich, ich bin noch klein;
   O mache mir das Herze rein;
   O bade mir die Seele hell
   In Deinem reichen Himmelsquell.

EIGHTEENTH- AND NINETEENTH-CENTURY GERMANY was very prolific in producing Christmas songs for children, much more than any other country. Written by parish priests and school-masters (who were required to be practising musicians), they were often tinged with sanctimoniousness. Not many could boast the genuine grace of this anonymous tune and poem.

Patapan

Burgundian, 17th century

translated by "O.B.C."

Bernard de la Monnoye (1641–1728)

R.F.

Wil - lie, take your lit - tle

Guil - lô, pran ton tam - bo -

2. Thus the men of olden days
   Loved the King of kings to praise:
   When they hear the fife and drum,
   Turelurelu, patapatapan,
   When they hear the fife and drum,
   Sure our children won't be dumb!

3. God and man are now become
   More at one than fife and drum.
   When you hear the fife and drum,
   Turelurelu, patapatapan,
   When you hear the fife and drum,
   Dance, and make the village hum!

THE OLDEST extant printed version of this carol appeared in 1842 in a volume entitled *Noëls bourguignons de Bernard de la Monnoye.* Our translation from the old Burgundian dialect was made by the editors of the *Oxford Book of Carols,* and our arrangement borrows some features from Martin Shaw's choral arrangement in the same book.

HOLD, MEN, HOLD!

Traditional English

Heavily

Hold, men, hold! We are ver-y cold, In - side and out - side,

we are ver - y cold. If you don't give us sil - ver,

then give us gold; From the mon - ey in your pock - ets, hold men, hold!

Traditional English
R.F.

THIS OLD MUMMERS' BEGGING SONG is distinctly for children. Never give them what they demand in this song until they have performed, as all good mummers should. Besides, they probably aren't really very cold.

SHEPHERDS WATCHED THEIR FLOCKS BY NIGHT

Pásli ovce valaši

Traditional Czech
translated by Mary Vojácek Cochrane

Traditional Czech
R.F.

Lively

1. Shep-herds watched their flocks by night Un-der Beth-'lem's stars so bright.
1. *Pás - li ov - ce va - la - ši, Při bet - lém - ské sa - la - ši.*

Hy - dom, hy - dom, tid - li - dom, Hy - dom, hy - dom, tid - li - dom.
Haj - dom, haj - dom, tyd - li - dom, Haj - dom, haj - dom, tyd - li - dom.

2. Came an angel telling them,
   They must go to Bethlehem.

3. "Hasten, hasten," they did say,
   "Jesus Christ you'll find this way."

4. Sleeping in a manger bare
   Lies the Holy Child so fair.

5. Mary rocks him tenderly,
   Joseph sings a lullaby:

2. *Andél se jim ukázal,*
   Do Betlému jít kázal.

3. *Jděte, jděte, prospěšte,*
   Pána Krista najdete.

4. *On tam leží v jesličkách,*
   Ovinutý v plenčičkách.

5. *Maria ho kolíbá,*
   Svatý Josef mu zpívá.

ONCE UPON A TIME, in the Carpathian ridge of eastern Moravia, there was a peaceful invasion of Italian and Roumanian shepherds. The Czech word for people of Latin origin at that time was *valaši;* and so the word gradually came to mean "shepherds" and the region was called Valassko. And that is the region where this simple carol about *valaši* is still sung today.

WASSAIL
SONG

Traditional English

Traditional English

R.F.

Gaily

D   Gmaj7   D   A7   D   A7   D

1.   Here we come a-was-sail-ing   A-mong the leaves so green, _____

2. We are not dai-ly beg-gars That beg from door to door, _____ But

G   D   A   A7   Emi   E   A7   D

Here _ we come a-wand'-ring, So fair ___ to be seen: Love and

we __ are neigh-bors' chil - dren Whom you have seen be - fore:

REFRAIN:

D   G   D   G   D

joy come to you,   And to you your was - sail too,   And God

bless you, and send __ you A hap - py new year, And God

send you A hap - py new year. _____

3. Call up the butler of this house,
   Put on his golden ring;
   Let him bring us a glass of beer,
   And better we shall sing:
   Refrain:

4. We have got a little purse
   Of stretching leather skin;
   We want a little money
   To line it well within:
   Refrain:

5. Bring us out a table,
   And spread it with a cloth;
   Bring us out a moldy cheese,
   And some of your Christmas loaf:
   Refrain:

6. God bless the master of this house,
   Likewise the mistress too;
   And all the little children
   That round the table go:
   Refrain:

7. Good Master and good Mistress,
   While you sit by the fire,
   Pray think of us poor children
   Awandering in the mire:
   Refrain:

IN THE 17TH CENTURY in the north of England, the probable time and origin of this carol, children went from door to door at Christmastime asking for handouts, much as American children do today at Halloween. The custom still prevails in many parts—though modern children seldom expect to be served beer.

For a grown-up's wassail song, see page 22.

SLEEP, MY LITTLE JESUS

William C. Gannett (1840–1923)

Adam Geibel (1855–1933)

H.W.S.

EXAMPLES of blind men who became successful musicians are rare, rarer still when they combine the career of church organist, composer, and publisher. Adam Geibel, born in Baden, Germany, was brought to Philadelphia at the age of seven, and attained all these distinctions, establishing a publishing house of his own in 1897. The words to his sweet lullaby, supposed to be sung by Mary, were written by a Unitarian minister from Rochester, N. Y.

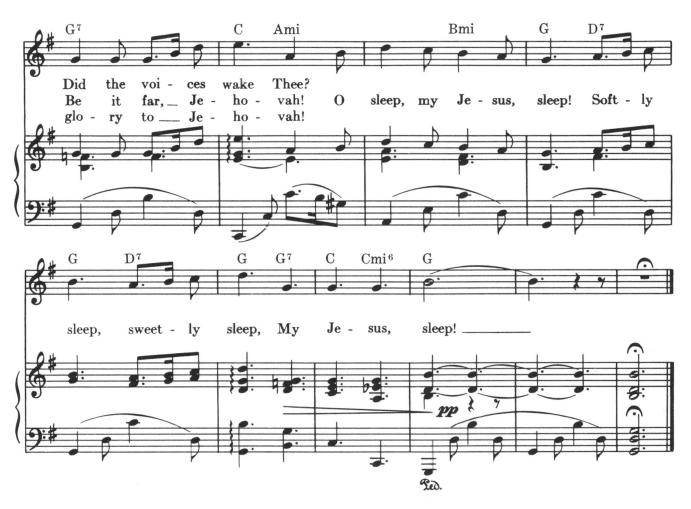

Did the voi - ces wake Thee?
Be it far, __ Je - ho - vah! O sleep, my Je - sus, sleep! Soft - ly
glo - ry to __ Je - ho - vah!

sleep, sweet - ly sleep, My Je - sus, sleep! _____

TO BETHL'EM I WOULD GO

Sel bych rád k Betlému

Traditional Czech
translated by Mary Vojácek Cochrane
Simply and not too fast

Traditional Czech
R.F.

To Beth - l'em I would go To Je - sus, He must know;
Sel bych rád k Be-tlé- mu, k Je - zí - sku ma - lé - mu

At __ home I have a black cock so __ trim, A cuck-oo both __ brown and __ slim,
Mám__ do __ ma kre-pe - li-cku a pe - knou ze-zu - li ___ cku,

These I will give to Him. Black cock will make Him gay,
ty mu o - dve - du. Bu - de ze - zu - li - cka

MRS. COCHRANE, who has translated many Czech folk songs, guesses that this carol probably comes from central or eastern Bohemia and that it may have been written for his pupils by one of the village schoolmasters. In Czechoslovakia these dominies were almost invariably well-trained musicians, for they were expected to help out with the church choir and even supply an occasional new hymn or processional. The same may be said of Austrian schoolmasters. (See note on *Silent Night*).

Once in Royal David's City

Henry John Gauntlett (1805–1876)

Cecil Frances Alexander (1823–1895)

R.F.

March time

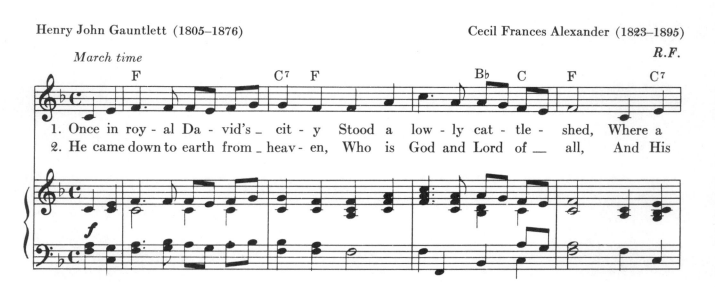

1. Once in roy - al Da - vid's _ cit - y Stood a low - ly cat - tle - shed, Where a
2. He came down to earth from _ heav - en, Who is God and Lord of _ all, And His

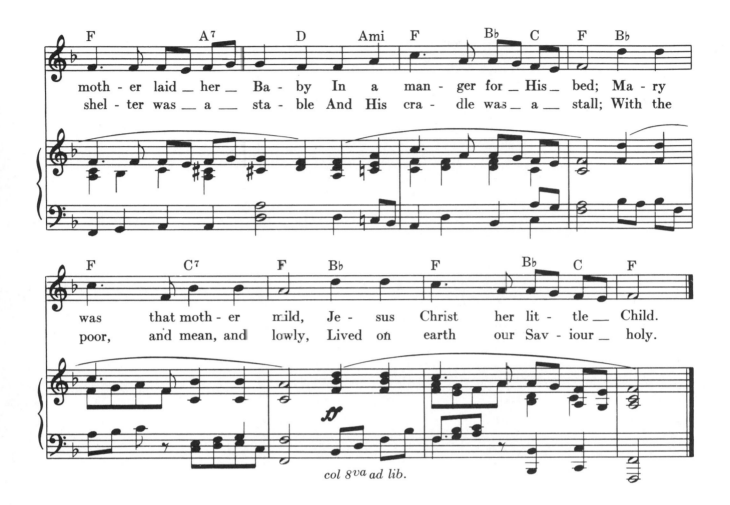

col 8va ad lib.

3. And, through all His wondrous childhood,
   He would honor, and obey,
   Love, and watch the lowly maiden
   In whose gentle arms He lay;
   Christian children all must be
   Mild, obedient, good as He.

4. For He is our childhood's pattern,
   Day by day like us He grew:
   He was little, weak, and helpless,
   Tears and smiles like us He knew;
   And He feeleth for our sadness,
   And He shareth in our gladness.

5. And our eyes at last shall see Him,
   Through His own redeeming love;
   For that Child so dear and gentle
   Is our Lord in heaven above;
   And He leads His children on
   To the place where He is gone.

6. Not in that poor lowly stable,
   With the oxen standing by,
   We shall see Him, but in heaven,
   Set at God's right hand on high;
   When like stars His children crowned,
   All in white shall wait around.

MRS. ALEXANDER, wife of the Primate of all Ireland, specialized in writing hymns for youngsters. Her most popular collection was one called *Hymns for Little Children* (1848) which achieved a record of over a hundred editions. This Christmas homily and the Easter homily *There Is a Green Hill Far Away* are the two poems from that collection which have survived most vigorously.

Henry Gauntlett, organist, organ designer, and composer, was even more prolific than his collaborator: he is said to have written over ten thousand hymn tunes. In its original form, the present tune (known in hymnals as IRBY) had an arrangement, like ours, for single voice and piano rather than for four voices, as it appears in all church anthologies.

WE THREE KINGS OF ORIENT ARE

John Henry Hopkins, Jr. (1820–1891)

John Henry Hopkins, Jr.

Simply and without dragging

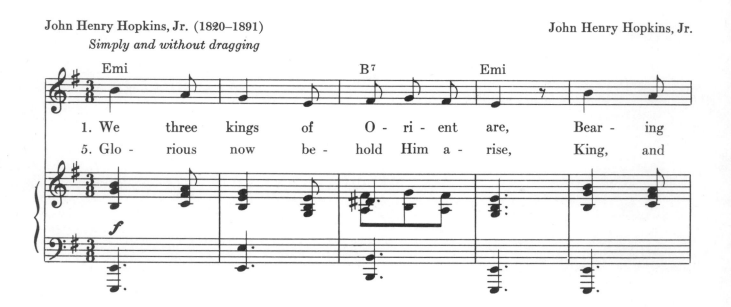

1. We three kings of O-ri-ent are, Bear - ing
5. Glo - rious now be - hold Him a - rise, King, and

Emi   B⁷   Emi   D

gifts   we   tra - verse a - far,   Field   and   foun - tain,
God,   and   sac - ri - fice;   Heaven   sings   al - le -

G   Ami   Emi   B⁷ Emi   D⁷

moor   and   moun - tain, Fol - low - ing yon - der star.
lu - ia: Al - le - lu - ia the earth   re - plies.   O —

189

Star of won - der, star of night, Star with roy - al beau - ty bright, West - ward lead - ing, still pro - ceed - ing, Guide us to thy per - fect light.

THE CAROL is not yet a century old; yet its style and mixture of modes have led a number of editors to believe it the work of a "medieval anon," and its composer and author to be credited merely as an "arranger." Hopkins, the son of the second Bishop of Vermont, was, as a matter of fact, a highly educated and versatile ecclesiastic. He was a poet of some note, a musicologist, a composer, and rector of various parishes. In his spare moments he designed stained-glass windows.

It is suggested that everyone join in on stanzas 1 and 5, and that individuals (preferably boys with unchanged voices) take the parts of Gaspar, Melchior, and Balthasar in the middle stanzas. With this in mind, we have supplied a heavier accompaniment for the first and last stanzas. But if the pianist finds the octaves a bit awkward, he can omit them—or else play the lighter arrangement for all five stanzas.

GASPAR. 2. Born a King on Beth - le - hem's plain, Gold I bring to
MELCHIOR. 3. Frank - in - cense to of - fer have I, In - cense owns a
BALTHASAR. 4. Myrrh is mine; its bit - ter per - fume Breathes a life of

crown Him a - gain, King for - ev - er, ceas - ing
De - i - ty nigh: Prayer and prais - ing all men
gath - er - ing gloom; Sor - rowing, sigh - ing, bleed - ing,

nev - er O - ver us all to reign. O _____
rais - ing, Wor - ship Him, God on high. O _____
dy - ing, Sealed in the stone - cold tomb. O _____

to Refrain

THE SEVEN JOYS OF CHRISTMAS

A group of high-school children

Traditional English
R.F.

Gaily

1. The first good joy that Christ-mas brings, It is the joy _ of one; _____ It
2. The next good joy that Christ-mas brings, It is the joy _ of two; _____ It

is to plan the Christ-mas gifts, And that is jol - ly fun._____ And
is to hang the stock-ings up Be - side the chim - ney flue. _____

that is jol - ly fun, good friends, So hap - py may we be, _____ And _____

sing the hope that Christ - mas joys May last e - ter - nal - ly. _____

The joy of three is to have old Santa Claus, that saint of jollity.
The joy of four is to see the Christmas tree, and toys upon the floor.
The joy of five is to welcome heartily the guests as they arrive.
The joy of six is to share the Christmas feast and in the sports to mix.
The joy of seven is the hope that all our lives the Christmas joys will leaven.

THE SEVEN JOYS OF MARY

1. The first good joy that Mary had,
   It was the joy of one;
   To see the blessed Jesus Christ
   When He was first her son:

REFRAIN:
   When He was first her son, good man,
   And blessed may He be,
   Both Father, Son, and Holy Ghost
   To all eternity.

The joy of two was to see her own son Jesus Christ
To make the lame to go.
The joy of three . . .
To make the blind to go.
The joy of four . . .
To read the Bible o'er.
The joy of five . . .
To bring the dead alive.
The joy of six . . .
Upon the crucifix.
The joy of seven . . .
To wear the crown of heaven.

MANY SETS of words have been sung to this gay little tune. The oldest and best-known version, *The Seven Joys of Mary,* dates from the 15th century; but as her "joy of six' sounds rather grim in the 20th century, I have given first a pleasantly naïve set of verses worked out fifty years ago by the second-year high-school class of the Ethical Culture School in New York City.

The tune is probably no older than the 18th century and has had many secular uses. London's unemployed, for example, sang it a hundred years ago to words beginning, "We've got no work to do-oo-oo." Not many years afterward, during a Connecticut childhood, my father and his playmates were piping it to this homiletic jingle:

   The man who hath plenty of fine peanuts
      And giveth his neighbor none,
   He shan't have any of my peanuts
      When his peanuts are gone.

SLEEP, MY SAVIOUR, SLEEP

Sabine Baring-Gould (1834–1924) Louise Reichardt (1788–1826)

Slowly, gently H.W.S.

1. Sleep, my Sav-iour, sleep, On Thy bed of hay; An-gels in the span-gled heav-en Sing their glad-some Christ-mas car-ols Till the break of day.

2. Sleep, my Sav-iour, sleep, Sweet on Ma-ry's breast, Now the shep-herds kneel a-dor-ing, Now the moth-er's heart is joy-ous, Take Thy hap-py rest.

NOVELIST, biographer, historian, musician, priest, and hymn-writer, Baring-Gould is most affectionately remembered as the author of *Now the Day Is Over* and *Onward, Christian Soldiers.* The last, like *Sleep, My Saviour, Sleep,* was intended for chil-dren to sing. I have adapted to Baring-Gould's verses a lullaby my German-born mother sang to me many years ago. It began *Schlaf', Kindlein, schlaf'.*

Christmas Solo Songs

OF THE FIFTY or more stage works composed by Adam, the only one that persistently keeps being performed is the ballet *Giselle*. But despite repeated attacks from ecclesiastical authorities on music (one French bishop denounced its "lack of musical taste and total absence of the spirit of religion"), *O Holy Night* remains, a century after its composition, easily the most popular Christmas solo song ever written. It has been arranged for all possible combinations of voices, even for an intimate madrigal group that published a recording a few years ago. Below I have contributed my mite in the form of a piano transcription. The translation by John Dwight, minister turned musical journalist, is practically a staple of American Christmas literature.

O HOLY NIGHT

Minuit, Chrétiens

Cappeau de Roquemaure

translated by John S. Dwight

Adolphe Charles Adam (1803–1856)

H.W.S.

With serenity

1. O ho - ly night! _____ the stars are bright - ly shin - ing, It is the night of the dear Sav - iour's birth!

2. Led by the light _____ of Faith se - rene - ly beam - ing, With glow - ing hearts by His cra - dle we stand.

Mi - nuit, Chré - tiens, _____ c'est l'heu - re so - len - nel - le Où l'hom - me Dieu des - cen - dit jus - qu'à nous,

He Shall Feed His Flock

Isaiah 40:11

Gently

George Frideric Handel (1685–1759)

H.W.S.

He — shall feed his flock like a

shep - herd, and He __ shall __ gath - er the lambs __ with __ His arm,

with _____ His arm. He __ shall feed his flock like a

shep - herd, and He __ shall __ gath - er the lambs __ with __ His arm,

with _____ His arm, and car - ry __ them __

THE TEXT for a number of Handel's oratorios was supplied the composer by a wealthy and conceited amateur named Charles Jennens. Jennens, in his turn, was supplied them, in all probability, by his secretary, a poor clergyman named Poole. The text for The *Messiah,* which came to Handel in this fashion, is a patchwork out of the Old and New Testaments. *He Shall Feed His Flock,* which comes from Isaiah, is the twenty-first, or penultimate, number in the first of the three parts of the oratorio, probably the most frequently performed oratorio in the history of music.

Our version follows the fashion in which the aria is most frequently sung in this country rather than the way it is commonly printed and the way Handel wrote it: that is, the first *He* is held for three eighths instead of just one, while *shall* gets just one instead of three. In a full performance, the aria has two stanzas. The first, in the key of F, as we have given it, is sung by the contralto; the second is sung a fourth higher, in the key of B-flat, by the soprano, with some alterations in the melody. Her words are based on Matthew 11:28–29 and run as follows: *Come unto Him, all ye that labor; come unto Him, all ye that are heavy laden, and He will give you rest. Take His yoke upon you, and learn of Him; for He is meek and lowly of heart, and ye shall find rest unto your souls.* In certain older copies, the soprano sang both parts in the higher key.

THE BIRTHDAY OF A KING

William Harold Neidlinger (1863–1924)

William Harold Neidlinger

R.F.

1. In the lit - tle vil - lage of
2. 'Twas a hum - ble birth-place, but

Beth - le - hem, There lay a Child one day, And the
oh! how much God gave to us that day, From the

sky was bright with a ho - ly light, O'er the place where Je - sus
man - ger bed, what a path has led, What a per - fect ho - ly

lay: Al - le - lu - ia! O how the an - gels sang, Al - le -
way: Al - le - lu - ia! O how the an - gels sang, Al - le -

lu - ia! how it rang; And the
lu - ia! how it rang; And the

205

COMPOSER, conductor, organist, Neidlinger gained an enviable reputation as a voice teacher in London, Paris, Chicago, and his native Brooklyn. He composed a number of comic operas and scores of songs; but his interests also lay in the psychology of pedagogics, and in East Orange, New Jersey, he founded a school for subnormal children. *The Birthday of a King* is the only example, in this book, of music of the drawing-room ballad type. It is included because no Christmas solo song, with the possible exceptions of Adam's *O Holy Night* and Handel's *He Shall Feed His Flock*, has had such wide popularity over so many years. It is now a mature sixty-five and still flourishes vigorously each December wherever a vocalist can find a pianist.

Eia, Eia

17th-century German
paraphrase by "A.G."

17th-century German
arranged by Johannes Brahms
H.W.S.

1. To us in Beth - lem cit - y Was born _ a lit - tle Son; In Him all gen - tle grac - es Were gath - ered in - to one,

all our love and for - tune Lie in _ his might - y hands; Our sor - rows, joys, and fail - ures, He sees _ and un - der - stands,

3. O Shepherd ever near us,
   We'll go where Thou dost lead;
   No matter where the pasture,
   With Thee at hand to feed,
   No matter where the pasture,
   With Thee at hand to feed,
   Eia, Eia,
   With Thee at hand to feed.

4. No grief shall part us from Thee,
   However sharp the edge:
   We'll serve, and do Thy bidding—
   O take our hearts in pledge!
   We'll serve, and do Thy bidding—
   O take our hearts in pledge!
   Eia, Eia,
   Take Thou our hearts in pledge!

Last time

2. And

BEGINNING with the German words *Zu Bethlehem geboren,* this carol first appeared in the *Cologne Psalter* in 1638. It was given its present, beautiful setting by Brahms to another set of traditional German words beginning *Die Blümelein sie schlafen* —also a lullaby but not a Christmas song. The Brahms adaptation of the tune is virtually the same as the original with the exception of his repetition of the first four bars. He dedicated it, along with a dozen other songs, to the children of his close friends, Robert and Clara Schumann, and called it *Sandmännchen.* Our sensitive and singable paraphrase is the work of a group of contributors to the *Oxford Book of Carols.* They modestly prefer to remain virtually anonymous.

THE HOLY BOY

Herbert S. Brown (1901–   )

John Ireland (1879–   )

H.W.S.

journ-ey'd far through the wild, __ Now wor-ship, si-lent, a - dor - ing, The

Boy, the Heav'n-ly Child _____ The Heav'n - ly Child! __

Leave your work and your play-time, And kneel in ho-mage and prayer, __ The

Prince of Love __ is smil-ing A-sleep in His cra - dle there! __

Bend your heart to the wond-er, The Birth, the Mys-te-ry mild, ___ And wor-ship, si-lent, a- dor-ing, The Boy, the Heav'n-ly Child ___ ___ The Heav'n-ly Child! ___ Dim the light of the lan-tern, And bare the mean ___ a- bode, ___ Yet gold and myrrh ___ and in-cense Pro-

COMPOSED DURING WORLD WAR I, John Ireland's music represents some of the less radical experimentation with dissonances and modal writing characteristic of his British compatriots. Today the music sounds almost classically simple, and its charm remains unimpaired. The piece was originally published in 1917 as one of a series of preludes for the piano.

Some twenty years later, writes Mr. Brown, Dr. Ireland asked him to try his hand at a set of verses for the Prelude. Mr. Brown, a solicitor in Kent, claims to be no poet. Yet, one Satur-

day at home, he admits, he "wrote the verses under the heavy influence of a cup of afternoon tea and a singularly tough currant bun." If one could generalize from this modest author's account, how simple it would be to evoke treasurable lyrics! Merely change the diet of a few lawyers.

My editing of the piano part represents a compromise between the Prelude, which carries a slightly different melody, and the composer's accompaniment to the song, which carries none.

CORNELIUS was a mid-nineteenth-century musical radical—that is, a devoted camp-follower of Liszt and of Wagner. He not only composed in the manner of Wagner's "music of the future," he also used his excellent literary gifts in the musical wars of the day. So radical were his practices, that the *première* of his one remembered opera, *The Barber of Baghdad,* led to Liszt's loss of his post as musical director of the opera house at Weimar.

Today the idiom of Cornelius can frighten no one. Yet, the freedom of its recitative-like voice line makes his lovely song the only one in our collection that we felt would be seriously damaged if arranged for piano solo. It comes from his Opus 8, *Weihnachtslieder,* a cycle of Christmas songs. The accompanying chorale is Nicolai's *How Brightly Shines the Morning Star,* which may be found with Bach's harmonization on page 132.

THE KINGS
Die Könige

Peter Cornelius (1824–1874)
translated by H. N. Bate

Peter Cornelius

King; Gold, in - cense, myrrh are their of - fer - ing.   2. The star shines
Gold Dem Kin - de __ spen - den zum Op - fer - sold.   2. *Und hell er -*

out __ with a stead-fast   ray;   The kings to Beth - le - hem make their way, And there in
glän - zet des Ster-nes   Schein;   Zum Stal-le ge - hen die Kön'ge   ein; Das Knäb-lein

wor - ship they bend the __ knee As   Ma - ry's Child __ in her __ lap they __ see;
schau - en sie won - nig - lich, An - be - tend nei -   gen die __ Kön' - ge __ sich;

Their roy - al gifts they show to the King; Gold, in-cense, myrrh are their of - fer - ing. __
Sie brin-gen Weih-rauch, Myrrhen und Gold zum Op - fer __ dar __ dem Knäb-lein __ hold. __

3. Thou child of man — lo, to Beth-le-hem The kings are trav'-ling—
3. *O Men-schen-kind! hal-te treu-lich Schritt! Die Kön'-ge wan-dern,—*

trav-el with them! The star of mer-cy, the star of
o wan-dre mit! Der Stern der Lie-be, der Gna-de
pick up the tempo slightly - - - -

grace, Shall lead thy — heart to its rest-ing place. Gold, in-cense, myrrh thou_ canst not—
Stern Er-hel-le dein Ziel, so du suchst den Herrn, Und feh-len Weih-rauch, Myrr-hen und

bring; Of-fer thy heart— to the in-fant— King, Of-fer thy heart!
Gold, Schen-ke dein Herz— dem— Knäb-lein— hold! Schenk' ihm dein Herz!

Christmas Rounds and Canons

WE WISH YOU A MERRY CHRISTMAS

Willys Peck Kent (1877–   )

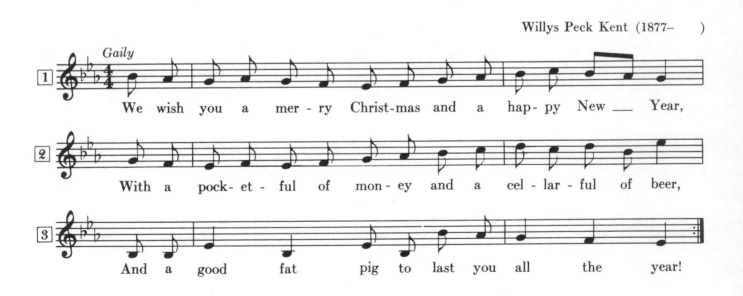

Gaily

1 We wish you a mer-ry Christ-mas and a hap-py New ___ Year,

2 With a pock-et-ful of mon-ey and a cel-lar-ful of beer,

3 And a good fat pig to last you all the year!

I LEARNED this round by rote in school some forty years ago. After writing it out from memory, I called Mr. Kent, who had taught it to me, to ask for its origin. He admitted to writing the music himself, the words having been supplied by a colleague, Miss Emma Mueden. He didn't know where she got them. Maybe Miss Mueden wrote them herself. They are certainly expressive of her cordial personality.

We Got a Lot for Christmas!

H.W.S.

Musikalischer Hausfreund, 1822

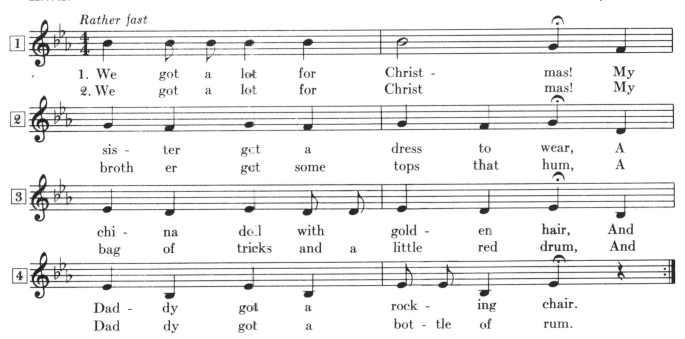

Rather fast

1. We got a lot for Christ - mas! My
2. We got a lot for Christ mas! My

sis - ter get a dress to wear, A
broth er got some tops that hum, A

chi - na doll with gold - en hair, And
bag of tricks and a little red drum, And

Dad - dy got a rock - ing chair.
Dad dy got a bot - tle of rum.

3. We got a lot for Christmas!
   My mother got the nicest thing,
   A pretty, shining diamond ring,
   And Daddy got the box and string.

4. We got a lot for Christmas!
   My sister and I got aches and chills,
   My mother has assorted ills,
   And Daddy's got to pay the bills.

THIS ROUND was entitled simply "December" when it appeared anonymously as the last of twelve—one for each month—in the annual *Musikalischer Hausfreund* of 1822. The single stanza, set to strictly even quarter notes, stated simply that Jesus would present drums and trumpets to little folk who had behaved nicely. It looked like a somewhat limited list to me, so I have paraphrased the original, adding a few stanzas and loosening the rhythm of the tune.

LULLY, LULLAY

Robert Croo (16th century)

Franz Josef Haydn (1732–1809)

1 Slowly

Lul - ly, lul - lay, _____ lul -

2

lay.
1. O sis - ters too, How may we
2. Her - od, the king, In his rag -
3. That woe is me, Poor child for

3

do For to pre - serve this day This poor young - ling For
ing, Charg - ed he hath this day All chil - dren young to
thee! And ev - er morn and day For thy part - ing to

4

whom we sing? By by, lul - lay.
slay, All child - ren young to slay.
say And sing, "By by lul - lay!"

HAYDN composed his poignant canon to the words of a German ditty beginning *Tod ist ein langer Schlaf* (Death is a long sleep). Our words are an adaptation of the tragic stanzas from the *Pageant of the Shearmen and Tailors* (see p. 27). For performance, it is suggested that each of the first three voices, upon completing all the words, begin at the beginning and hum the music until the last voice has sung all the words. At that point, the initial chord should be hummed very softly.

Christmas Eve Canon

H.W.S.

Franz Josef Haydn (1732–1809)

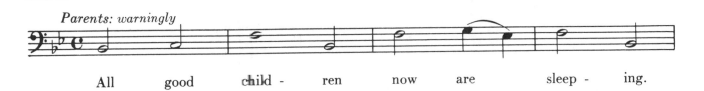

Parents: warningly

All good child - ren now are sleep - ing.

Children 1: gleefully

We can - not sleep at all, Come, let us quick - ly crawl,

Children 2:

Please do not be so cross, We will just wake and toss,

Parents:

All good child - ren

to 2

Creep soft - ly down the hall — Do let us see!

to 1

Dream - ing of San - ta Claus And his Christ-mas tree.

now are sleep - ing.

THE PARENTS (or, at least, the fathers) should sing the first line alone and then keep on repeating it so long as the children keep up their two-part round.

Haydn's music, known as the *Nightingale Canon*, was written as a round for treble voices only. That is authority enough for letting mothers sing the first line too, one octave higher.

THREE SACRED CANONS

Alleluia

Wolfgang Amadeus Mozart (1756–1791)
adapted by Harry R. Wilson

Dona Nobis Pacem

Composer unknown

NONE of these three canons was written to words intended specifically for Christmas; yet people love to sing them especially at that time. Therefore they are given here all in the same key so that they can be sung one after another without stopping.

Mozart, like most of the great German composers, wrote a large number of canons for his friends. One of them is a fine but very difficult *Alleluia*. I have therefore substituted an adaptation made by my good friend Professor Harry R. Wilson of Columbia University. It is based on the coloratura aria from the motet *Exultate* and faithfully preserves both the harmonies and the voice-lines of that famous work.

Ave Maria

Wolfgang Amadeus Mozart (1756–1791)

A - - ve Ma - ri - a, A - - - - ve _ Ma - ri - a.

A - - ve, A - - ve _ Ma - ri - a.

A - - ve Ma - ri - a, Ma - ri - - a, A -

- - ve. A - ve Ma - ri - a, A - - ve, A - - ve.

Christmas Is Coming

English nursery rhyme

Edith Nesbitt

Christ - mas is com - ing, The goose is get - ting fat;

Please to put a pen - ny in the old man's ___ hat,

Please to put a pen - ny in the old man's ___ hat.

THIS GAY and quickly learned round is often used while the hat
is being passed for some holiday collection.

Will I Get a Christmas Present?

H.W.S.

Franz Josef Haydn (1732–1809)

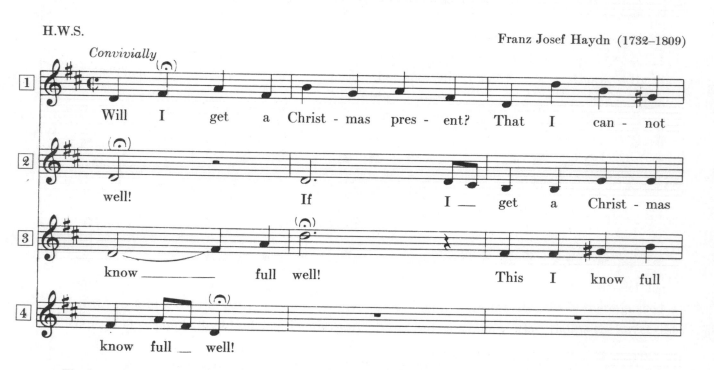

Will I get a Christ - mas pres - ent? That I can - not well! If I _ get a Christ - mas know _ full well! This I know full know full _ well!

The first voice should sing all the way through the lines marked 1. Then, when he begins with the lines marked 2, the second voice begins with 1. The third voice begins with 1 when the first begins 3, and so forth.

The holds (⌢) indicate the place where Haydn suggested that the round end. That is, whoever is singing the first line, holds on to the word "I" on the F-sharp; the other three hold on to the word "well" on the D indicated.

You will find it all much simpler than these directions may sound.

tell.   If I get a Christ - mas pres - ent,

pres - ent,   If I get a Christ - mas

well!   If I get a Christ - mas

If I real - ly get a pres - ent, I will real - ly

(begin 2)

I will real - ly not de - serve it: This __ I __ know full

(begin 3)

pres - ent, I will real - ly not de - serve it: This I

(begin 4)

pres - ent, I will real - ly not de - serve it:__ This I

(begin 1)

not de - serve it: This I know full well!

THE UNRHYMED tavern song to which Haydn set his jolly round is slightly more philosophical but hardly less greedy than our recollection of childhood anticipations. It begins: *Ob ich morgen leben werde,* and may be freely rendered:

> If I'll be alive tomorrow,
> This I cannot tell;
> Yet if I'm alive tomorrow,
> Drink will surely drown my sorrow:
> This I know full well.

ON THE CORNER

H.W.S.

French-Canadian

March time

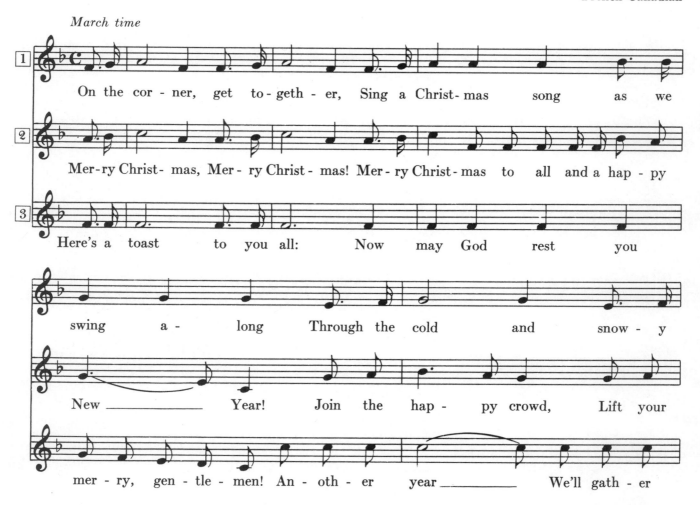

On the cor-ner, get to-geth-er, Sing a Christ-mas song as we

Mer-ry Christ-mas, Mer-ry Christ-mas! Mer-ry Christ-mas to all and a hap-py

Here's a toast to you all: Now may God rest you

swing a - long Through the cold and snow-y

New _____ Year! Join the hap - py crowd, Lift your

mer-ry, gen - tle - men! An - oth - er year _____ We'll gath - er

ABOUT CHRISTMAS of 1925 in Paris, a French-Canadian intro-duced this round to a group of friends, and we used to chant it marching along the boulevards. The words had nothing whatso-ever to do with Christmas: in a tough French-Canadian dialect they told a rather rowdy story about a cocoa-peddler named Rampollo. The following year I introduced it to the glee club of the University of Tennessee to words appropriate for a football song, under the title of "Tennessee, Suh!" Now it has struck me as a useful round for carolers as they go from one door to the next, and so I have concocted this new set of verses.

weath - er, March - ing up and down a - round the town. **to 2**

voic - es loud, And we'll soon find you a cup of cheer! **to 3**

here, And then we'll all be toast - ing you a - gain! **to 1**

Canon of the Mimes

H.W.S.   Michael Praetorius (1571–1621)

Moderately

1. Hear the mimes! In

2. old - en times And

3. for - eign climes They

4. sang their rhymes.

5. Ring, Christ - mas

6. chimes!

IN THE MIDDLE AGES mummers, or mimes, not only presented plays at Christmastime, but also went about town in costume, serenading houses where they were likely to receive handouts. Another word for them, when they only sing and do not act, is *waits*. The custom, of course, still persists.

"Praetorius" is a Latinization of "Schultze" adopted by no fewer than five 16th- and 17th-century German composers. Michael, the great theoretician, published over twenty-five volumes of works during his lifetime, and is beloved by all carol singers for his harmonization of *Lo, How a Rose E'er Blooming* (see p. 84). Our six-part, six-measure canon is one of scores that he composed.

MASTERS IN THIS HALL

Canonic version

William Morris (1834–1896)

Old French
H.W.S.

Now - ell! Now - ell! Now - ell! Now - ell sing we clear! Hol - pen

pray: Now - ell! Now - ell! Now - ell! Now - ell sing we

ev - er I you pray: Now - ell! Now - ell! Now - ell!

sea, _____ And ev - er I you pray: Now - ell! Now - ell!

are all folk on earth, _ Born _ is God's son so dear:

clear! Hol - pen are all folk on earth, _ Born _ is God's son so

Now - ell sing we clear! Hol - pen are all folk on earth, _ Born _

Now - ell! Now - ell sing we clear! Hol - pen are all folk on

dear:

is God's son so dear:

earth, _ Born _ is God's son so dear: _____

WITH ONE minor alteration in the
tune, this fine, vigorous carol is here
presented as a strict canon. True, it
was never intended to be a canon, and
it breaks some of the laws of good
canonic writing. For example, two of
the voices sometimes find themselves
singing in unison. This may be avoided
by using only two parts, preferably di-
vided between bass and treble; however, four parts make for more noise
and more fun. For a more conventional
arrangement, see page 36.

O, HOW LOVELY IS THE EVENING
O wie wohl ist's mir am Abend

Quietly

O, how love-ly is the eve-ning, is the eve-ning,
O wie wohl ist's mir am A - bend, mir am A - bend,

When the bells are sweet-ly ring-ing, sweet-ly ring-ing,
Wenn zur Ruh' die Glok-ke läu-tet, Glok-ke läu-tet,

Ding, dong, ding, dong, ding, dong.
Bim, bam, bim, bam, bim, bam.

ONE OF THE SIMPLEST and sweetest rounds ever written. Not strictly a Christmas round, it can be made one by singing the second line: *When the Christmas bells are ringing,* or, in German: *Wenn die Weihnachtsglocken läuten.*

Merry Christmas

Sarah C. Fouser (1889–   )

Charles E. Fouser (1889–1946)

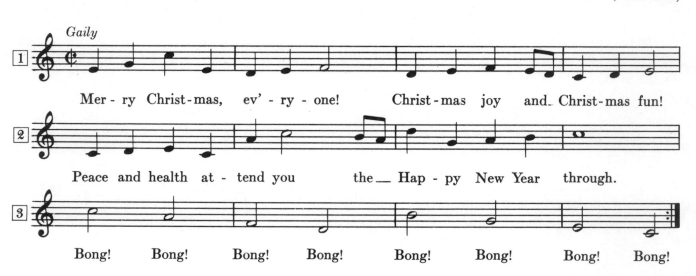

Gaily

Mer-ry Christ-mas, ev'-ry-one! Christ-mas joy and Christ-mas fun!

Peace and health at-tend you the Hap-py New Year through.

Bong! Bong! Bong! Bong! Bong! Bong! Bong! Bong!

COMPOSER, organist, and educator, Professor Fouser spent the last fifteen years of his life teaching at Northern Illinois State Teachers College in De Kalb. Each year he and his gifted wife used to send their friends musical Christmas greetings of their own composition. This particular round was the Christmas greeting for 1936.

GLORY TO GOD
Ehre sei Gott

Ludwig Ernst Gebhardi (1787–1862)

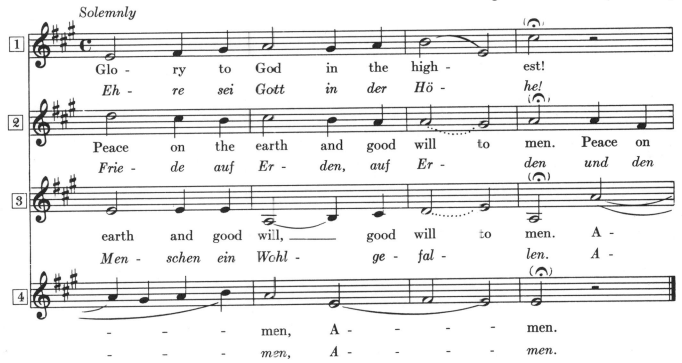

Solemnly

1 Glo - ry to God in the high - est!
Eh - re sei Gott in der Hö - he!

2 Peace on the earth and good will to men. Peace on
Frie - de auf Er - den, auf Er - den und den

3 earth and good will, _____ good will to men. A -
Men - schen ein Wohl - ge - fal - len. A -

4 - - - men, A - - - men.
- - - men, A - - - men.

GEBHARDI was one of the thoroughly trained musicians that Germany produced in abundance a hundred years and more ago. His textbook in harmony, which he used with his classes at the Erfurt Seminary, featured the writing of canons, and this is one of his own numerous excellent examples.

The round may be stopped at the end of any given line.

233

INDEXES

INDEX OF TITLES AND FIRST LINES

English titles are printed in capitals (A BABE IS BORN), *first lines in capitals and lower case* (All good children now are sleeping). *Foreign-language titles and first lines are printed in italics* (Adeste, fideles). *When titles and first lines are the same, they are given only once.*

INDEX OF MUSICAL AND LITERARY SOURCES